FRUIT AND VEGGIES 101 SUMMER FRUITS

GARDENING GUIDE ON HOW TO GROW THE FRESHEST & RIPEST SUMMER FRUITS (PERFECT FOR BEGINNERS) INCLUDES - FRUIT SALAD, SMOOTHIES & FRUIT JUICES RECIPES

GREEN ROOTS

Fruit and Veggies 101

SUMMER FRUITS

Gardening Guide On How To Grow The Freshest & Ripest Summer Fruits

(Perfect For Beginners)

INCLUDES: FRUIT SALAD, SMOOTHIES & FRUIT JUICES RECIPES

GREEN ROOTS

CONTENTS

A SPECIAL GIFT TO OUR READERS

Included with your purchase of this book is our list of "27 horticulture Myths Debunked"
This list will provide and aid you as a new (or soon-to-be) gardener by actively informing you of the myths and irrelevant practices to avoid during your gardening journey.

Visit the link below to let us know which email address to deliver to

www.gardengreenroots.com

INTRODUCTION

Growing your garden fruits can be an enriching experience. You have the pleasure of watching your favorite fruits grow and thrive because of your efforts, and you can also reap the benefits of consuming pesticide-free and fresh produce. Not only do the fruits taste better when they are freshly picked, but they are also much more nutritious than store-bought produce that may have been sitting in storage for days or genetically modified fruits.

The advantages of growing your garden fruits are plentiful. From the apparent health benefits of consuming fresh and nutritious produce to growing something with your hands, gardening is a gratifying experience. Not only will it provide you with delicious fruits, but it can also be a great source of exercise and stress relief.

On top of all this, cultivating your home garden allows you to save money on expensive store-bought produce while becoming more environmentally conscious by using fewer outsourced resources. With so many positive outcomes, it's no surprise more individuals and families are taking advantage of growing their garden fruits for a healthier life physically, financially, nutritionally, and mentally.

RECLAIM AND REVITALIZE YOUR WELL-BEING WITH GARDENING

With the pressures brought on by today's society, alongside the fast-paced and hectic world we live in, it's easy to forget to take a break and prioritize ourselves. Quite a few of us are at fault of this.

It is fair to recognize that as individuals, our life responsibilities differ from our peers and counterparts; whether it may be raising children, family obligations, or work commitments, the list can go on. However, how do we ensure we have the capacity and capability to fulfill our responsibilities when we feel physically, mentally, and emotionally depleted? Some of us don't have a medium or haven't recognized why having one is essential to reclaiming and revitalizing your well-being.

Thankfully, reclaiming and revitalizing your well-being is within reach. Gardening provides a sense of tranquillity while taking productivity to the next level - think therapeutic relaxation plus tangible results. Cultivating your well-being never felt so good.

Gardening can be one of the most effective ways to reclaim your sense of well-being and rejuvenate your mental, physical, and emotional health. Whether you create an urban enclave or tend to a sprawling backyard garden, many cultures worldwide have embraced gardening as an essential part of living a holistic lifestyle. Not only does gardening bring people closer to nature and help connect us with our creativity, but it also produces tangible fruits and vegetables that nourish us from the inside out.

Gardening has proven on numerous occasions the therapeutic and rewarding benefits it has to offer. It's been proven in science, in our communities, and it is becoming common knowledge season by season. It's an engaging pursuit that requires physical effort, attention to detail, and patience. Besides, it is an ideal way to reconnect with nature or spend time doing something productive.

The act of tending to plants brings peace amidst stress and can help us reclaim our well-being. For example, spending time in the garden encourages mindfulness, which allows us as a gardener to take in our surroundings and appreciate nature's beauty more deeply than ever before. By providing healthy living, entertainment, and education all at once, it is no wonder why gardening has proven so rewarding - it satisfies both mind and body.

Creating beauty in the garden allows reflection and can provide moments of clarity or contentment. Not only is it great for mental health, but it also gives us a sense of accomplishment, which enhances self-satisfaction and boosts morale while providing exercise along the way.

Gardening rejuvenates our spirit and replenishes our soul —bringing a balance between mind, body, heart, and nature that we all need in this day and age.

As the saying goes, "Hiding in plain sight"; gardening has been a centuries-old practice of self-care and well-being yet is often underestimated or overlooked. This time-tested activity remains an invaluable way to prioritize your health by communing with nature in the comfort of your home. In other words, you don't have to look far for relief.

What You Can Expect To Learn

In this book, you will learn all there is to know about fruit gardening. This beginner-friendly guide offers comprehensive knowledge on how to create a garden that flourishes with fruity deliciousness. Within its pages, you'll get actionable steps and techniques best suited for your gardening aims and goals, from selecting the best-growing soil and prepping your gardening space to successfully harvesting your summer fruits for the perfect fruit salad.

The fruits you will learn to plant and grow successfully are raspberries, pears, apples, strawberries, kiwis, watermelon, oranges, and grapes.

In this guide, we also want to take it a step further and provide additional guidance on how to make the most of your freshest harvested summer fruits, from guides and recipes on creating your very own juicy and flavourful fruit salads, smoothies, and fruit juices.

Creating your own fruit salad, smoothies, and fruit juices with the fruits grown from your garden is a great way to experience the incredible flavor that comes from harvesting your organic produce. It can be a very rewarding experience to savor the subtle taste and texture of freshly-picked fruits you've gathered by hand, and they bring beautiful colors and smells to your kitchen.

Not only that, but with a garden's worth of fresh ingredients, you can create some truly delicious combinations of flavors and textures in your fruit salads, smoothies, and fruit juices you'd never find in store-bought versions.

Why This Book Is Exactly What You Need

You may question whether this is the right book to guide you into and along your fruit gardening journey. The good news is that we can confidently assure you that this is the perfect guide to do so.

Why are we confident, some may ask? Because at Green Roots, we have been fortunate to reap, explore and discover the rewards of gardening, with 20 years of collective gardening knowledge and experience.

Our primary mission is to equip gardeners worldwide with the necessities and skills to cultivate their own fruit gardens, and that's precisely what we have done in this guide. We will show you all the successful tips and tricks we have used over the years, especially those we have used to maintain long-term gardens.

Gardening is one of the most enjoyable and rewarding hobbies however, too often people are convinced that they don't have the knowledge or skills to grow fruits successfully in their homes. A big part of this common assumption is the highly decorated myths and misconceptions associated with fruit gardening.

A typical example is the belief that a fruit garden requires a large space to cultivate successfully when in reality, many small gardens can be planted in square-foot boxes, larger raised beds, and containers.

So, whether you're an experienced gardener that wants to freshen up their skills or a complete beginner looking to start from scratch, this guide will not only dispel such gardening myths but will provide you with clear, accurate, and easy-to-follow steps that show how simple planting, maintaining and harvesting fruits can be.

We have not just worked on our fruit gardens over the years, but we have been fortunate to witness the power of gardening and how it has transformed the lives of others by simply understanding how to cultivate for themselves, and it brings us joy to know many more will be able to reap the full benefits of fruit and vegetable gardening.

So let the journey begin!

CHAPTER 1
YOUR GROWING SPACE: PREPARATION AND TECHNIQUES

Remember how we told you that there are various misconceptions and myths about growing a fruit garden? Well, the same can be said about myths surrounding where one should grow their fruit garden.

What really matters when choosing an area to plant your first fruit trees is the local climate and the available space – that will dictate what fruits do best in any given environment.

With the right resources and knowledge, anyone can start a fruit garden no matter what constraints they believe prove otherwise. All you need is an open mind and patience—if applied correctly, your efforts will be rewarded with fresh fruits of your choosing.

So don't let any myths about where or how one should grow, deter you from taking up this rewarding activity—you just need to arm yourself with the necessary guidance for success. Fortunately, that's precisely what you've done already.

CHOOSE WHERE YOUR FRUIT GARDEN WILL GROW

Starting a fruit garden is an exciting endeavor, but first, you'll need to choose a space or location to plant your fruits. While many associate fruit gardens with large plots in yards or fields outside, this isn't always an option for everyone, nor necessarily the best choice given the individual living situations and available space.

Whether it's in your backyard or even indoors, inspecting your home environment can help you decide which type of gardening arrangement will work best - providing ample opportunities for successful fruit growing. Take time to explore all possibilities, ensuring you pick one that best fits your living environment's size and capabilities.

Growing a luscious and productive fruit garden can be done in numerous ways. Whether you choose to use raised beds, containers, or the traditional in-ground method, we've got all bases covered here. We'll provide an overview of each style – outlining the significant benefits and drawbacks with each – so that you find yourself well-equipped to make your own gardening decisions.

IN-GROUND FRUIT GARDENING

Growing your own fruit can be a rewarding experience for gardeners. One of the most popular ways to do so is through the in-ground growing method. By choosing the right spot for your garden, providing ample sunshine and water, and taking care of the soil, you can watch your fruit transform from a seed or cutting into a bountiful harvest.

There are several advantages to an in-ground growing method over other methods like planting containers; it costs less overall while increasing yield and drought tolerance and encouraging healthy amounts of pollinating insects around your garden, which help increase yield further. With proper planning and care, you can enjoy homegrown fruits with minimal effort.

Advantages of In-Ground Gardening

- Growing fruit in the ground allows for better root and soil aeration, leading to larger and healthier fruits.
- The soil heats up quicker than raised beds or pots, allowing for a quicker harvest of your fruits.
- With in-ground gardening, plants are less prone to being attacked by pests or diseases because their roots have access to soil minerals that create a stronger immune system.
- The soil depth in an in-ground garden is greater than in raised beds or pots. As a result, it retains more moisture during dry spells.
- Fruits grown in this environment tend to be heartier and more flavourful due to added exposure to the elements.
- An organized garden layout allows for easier harvesting and succession planting of crops.
- It will cost less money to set it up.

Disadvantages of In-Ground Gardening

- One significant disadvantage of in-ground gardening is the increased exposure to weeds and

pests. Weeds can choke out healthy plants by
taking all the nutrients and sunlight available.

- Unlike container gardening or raised bed gardens,
  in-ground gardens require more digging and
  preparation, which can be challenging when
  dealing with tougher soils or climates.
- If soil quality is terrible, creating healthy soil may
  require a lot of investment.
- The soil may get too bulky and dense, causing
  slow water drainage.

CONTAINER FRUIT GARDENING

Utilizing containers to grow your fruits is a simple way to
add more produce to your diet. The ability to easily track
the growth of each plant allows for better monitoring of
your fruits, and you can use this information to ensure you
are getting the maximum benefit from their development.

Containers also allow for easier picking and harvesting
when your fruits are ripe. You can easily reposition or
move them with increased mobility to capture even more
sunlight or ensure they don't get too much water.

All in all, using containers to grow your fruits provides an
excellent opportunity for those who want to take control of
the quality and quantity of their food.

Advantages of Container Gardening

- Container gardening provides its users the ability
  to move their plants with ease.
- It's easy to control the soil temperature and
  moisture levels, which can ensure better fruit

production, healthier and larger fruits, as well as improved flavor.

- With container gardening, you don't have to worry about weeds or pests, making it easier to maintain than other types of gardens.
- Containers create good drainage so water can move freely throughout the root system.
- You can buy good and treated soil ready to use for containers.
- It's easy to set up.
- There are fewer chances of soil compaction.

Disadvantages of Container Gardening

- Smaller containers mean the plants must be confined, adversely affecting their overall growth and production of fruit.
- Overcrowded containers can make it difficult to protect from pests, as the root structure of dense plants can attract insects and other animals that may damage or destroy crops.
- Roots can be compressed with little space to grow.

RAISED BED FRUIT GARDENING

Gardening in raised beds is an innovative way of growing fruits. It allows for greater control over soil conditions and can be tailored to the specific requirements of different plants. A carefully designed system will enable fruits to be grown with minimal space and maximum yields.

This gardening method involves using a predefined space, such as a frame or wall with soil inside, allowing the plants to be planted at the desired level above ground.

The main benefit of raised bed gardening is increased air circulation and drainage, which promotes healthier plants and more successful harvests. As a whole growing fruit in raised beds is an excellent way for gardeners of all levels to produce incredibly delicious yields.

Advantages of Raised Bed Gardening

- With soil above ground level and beds at waist height, raised beds make it easier to stay physically active in the garden without hunching or kneeling when planting and weeding.
- The soil in a raised bed holds moisture better than traditional ground plots, which makes it easier to control water levels and keep plants hydrated.
- Raised beds can be built anywhere, so they are ideal for growing fruits on terraces and rooftops and in small yards with limited space.
- There's virtually no weed infestation.
- You can easily control the quality of your soil from the start.
- It can be simple to set up pre-made raised beds.

Disadvantages of Raised Bed Gardening

- It can be expensive to buy all the materials to construct a raised bed, such as soil and compost, as well as the lumber for the structure. This is not ideal for someone who may have just started gardening and may not have much money to invest in materials.
- They can't be moved around like containers.

ESSENTIALS TOOLS AND EQUIPMENT FOR BEGINNERS

Fruit gardening is an enjoyable and rewarding activity that anyone can partake in. Still, it pays to understand and use the correct gardening tools and equipment to make it even more successful.

Included are a wide range of products such as spades, shovels, hoes, rakes, wheelbarrows, and garden shears. Each tool serves a distinct purpose when cultivating fruit gardens - from digging and cultivating soil to watering, trimming plants, or removing weeds.

It's also essential to select the right tool for the job for improved accuracy. Utilizing the appropriate tools can significantly reduce the amount of backbreaking work involved in growing fruit gardens, as well as reducing preparation time, enabling you to spend more hours enjoying your outdoor masterpiece.

The correct tools allow you to work more quickly, efficiently, and correctly. Without them, the results could be disastrous. Furthermore, if the proper instruments are not used for maintenance and upkeep, it could lead to diseases in your plants or other unwanted effects that reduce productivity or threaten their health altogether.

That is why it is important for gardeners of all skill levels to understand and use gardening tools correctly - you don't want little mistakes from improper use leading to bigger problems in the future.

BEGINNER GARDENING TOOLS

Pruning Shears

Whether you're a professional gardener or a backyard fruit enthusiast, it's critical to understand the importance of using pruning shears on your plants. With regular maintenance through pruning, gardens are more productive and aesthetically pleasing.

Pruning shears allow you to get rid of dead, diseased, and damaged branches and ensure that your plants are growing in the right direction. Removing unwanted growth, such as new shoots or suckers, allows the plant to direct its energy toward producing sweet fruits instead of maintaining leaves that may not serve any purpose.

Pruning helps facilitate better airflow and sun access to promote healthier produce and gives shape to your shrubs and trees for a charming landscape.

In addition, pruning shears are great for gathering flowering and fruiting material that can then be used to fertilize the garden. When investing in quality tools like pruning shears, gardeners can achieve larger fruits with greater garden yields.

Garden Wheelbarrow

A garden wheelbarrow is a tool that provides immense value to any fruit gardener. It can quickly and easily transport larger loads of soil, fertilizer, and weeds and helps protect your back from the strain associated with carrying heavy loads.

Its ability to be moved over any terrain, whether grass or uneven ground, allows for more efficient transport of materials. Additionally, it prevents soil compaction. The narrow surface area of the single wheel doesn't disturb existing roots when moving around the garden.

Overall, having a Garden Wheelbarrow on hand is essential for any serious fruit gardener who needs an easier way to move materials that simply cannot be carried by hand. Having a wheelbarrow in your garden inventory will prove its value in no time.

Watering Cans

Using a watering can is essential for fruit gardens as it allows for precise water delivery and helps to ensure that plants and tsrees get only the desired amount of moisture they need.

Watering cans are beneficial in areas that have frequent dry spells or limited rainfall since they can save valuable time, labor, and resources. Hand watering with a watering can also allow gardeners to observe their fruit gardens more closely and spot potential problems such as disease, pests, or nutrient deficiencies. All in all, there's no worthwhile substitute for a trustworthy watering can in any fruit garden.

Garden Rake

Gardens providing fruits are very beneficial, as they provide essential nutrients and energy for our bodies. However, ensuring a successful fruit garden requires more than just planting and harvesting the plants.

Using a garden rake is vital for soil health and good plant growth. A garden rake helps remove stones and debris between the tilled soil without disturbing its structure. It also levels any lumps or bumps while raking over the soil surface, which allows air circulations to occur, resulting in the roots being able to breathe better.

Moreover, it can help break up any compaction by loosening the hard soils so plant roots can easily penetrate and receive adequate water flow throughout the area. Without using a garden rake regularly in a fruit garden, it would be challenging to create an optimum growing environment for healthy harvests of fruits.

Garden Hoe

Using a garden hoe is an essential tool for maintaining fruit gardens. The hoe can be used to turn the soil, which helps to aerate it and provides better drainage. This also encourages deeper root growth, meaning plants can access more water and nutrients for healthy fruit production.

Additionally, a garden hoe can help protect gardens from harmful pests by loosening the soil and allowing it to dry out between waterings, creating an inhospitable environment for many types of insects.

Finally, hoes are great tools for cultivating weeds - simply draw the blade across the soil's surface to remove unwanted plants without resorting to chemicals or manual plucking.

All in all, using a garden hoe is vital for keeping your fruit garden looking its best and producing delicious fruits. With a quality garden hoe, these important jobs become much easier and keep your fruit garden well maintained so your crops can thrive throughout the season.

Garden Spade

A garden spade is essential for fruit gardens since it allows the soil to be dug up and manipulated much easier than other tools. By stirring and turning the soil, you can help replenish the nutrients in the soil and also provide oxygen to the root systems of the plants.

Having a spade or shovel at your disposal makes it much easier to create a deeper layer of topsoil by digging deeply into the top layers and allowing beneficial nutrients from lower down in the earth to work its way up.

Using a garden spade could also be useful for moving large yard debris due to its size and shape. Lastly, using a garden spade helps with aeration, which is an essential factor when it comes to having healthy soil that will result in healthier fruits growing in your garden.

Gardening Gloves

Garden gloves are a critical aspect of safe and successful fruit gardening. They protect the hands from the sharp thorns of many fruiting shrubs and bushes, as well as from contact with chemical pesticides and fertilizers.

Wearing garden gloves makes it easier to grasp weeds and other plants when weeding or pruning, allowing for more precise movements that do less damage to surrounding plants. Additionally, garden gloves protect skin from dirt and bacteria - all too often overlooked in a fruit garden, leading to diseases that create serious issues.

With so many benefits, investing in a sturdy pair of garden gloves is wise before starting on any important horticultural task.

Garden Trug

A garden Trug is a versatile and essential tool for any fruit garden. Its lightweight material and deep sides make it invaluable for those looking to safely transport fruit, plants, and garden prunings without damage.

Whether harvesting apples, transporting seedlings, or dealing with the aftermath of pruning, a Trug will help keep your fruits safe at every stage of the gardening process. The tool's deep sides also provide extra stability when deadheading or harvesting heavy crops, while its flat base helps reduce stress on your back by providing support as you stoop low to reach underhand.

Finally, the durable construction means it can last through many seasons of hard work, making it an ideal planting accessory for beginners and seasoned tenders alike.

THE BASICS OF GARDEN SOIL PREPARATION

Fruit gardening is a wonderful way to get outside and enjoy nature while producing sweet and delicious fruits. However, successfully growing fruit in the garden requires an understanding of the soil type being used for planting.

Soil to plants is equivalent to the air humans need to live and thrive. Plants require soil, and not just any soil, but healthy soil. It must be rich in all of the minerals necessary to grow substantial and nutritious fruit plants. It is common to believe that all soils are healthy; however, this is not the case.

You cannot expect vigorous growth from your garden if it has not been prepared correctly for fruit plants. Different types of soils exist depending on the climate, location, and landscape of where you live.

All these aspects greatly influence how well fruits can be produced. Some soils are made up of different textures, like heavy clay or light sand, while others contain more organic matter, such as compost and mulch.

Each soil type has different needs concerning water, drainage, pH levels, and nutrient availability. If you know what kind of soil you have and its characteristics, you can adjust conditions in the garden so that plants are producing healthy fruits in no time.

FIVE TYPES OF GARDEN SOIL

Silt Soil: Silt soil is a type of soil made up of fine sedimentary particles. It is not as sandy or gravelly as other types of soil, and as a result it can provide good support for small and delicate fruit trees.

Silt soil has the benefit of excellent drainage, meaning that any water that accumulates during rainstorms will easily be able to run off and won't pool around the roots, resulting in potential rot.

In addition, silt soil tends to warm quickly in the spring, allowing fruit trees to begin flowering earlier in the season. However, one disadvantage of silt soil is its low ability to retain nutrients, meaning gardeners wishing to grow fruits successfully may need to supplement the soil with regular fertilizer applications.

Additionally, this type of soil is prone to drying out more quickly than other soils; therefore, special attention must be paid when watering these fruit trees from late spring through fall.

Clay Soil: Clay soil is a type of soil that is made up of tiny particles, which form together and create a densely packed substrate that can be difficult to penetrate.

Despite this difficulty, clay soil can help to support healthy fruit gardening due to its strong nutrient retention capabilities, allowing it to lock in essential substances and help them reach the plant's roots more effectively.

However, clay soil also has its downsides; because it clumps together, it does not absorb water particularly well and can cause drainage issues for young plants. Furthermore, as it retains nutrients, if too many are added over time, they can build up in the ground and poison the soil, making it hard for all vegetation to thrive.

Overall, clay soil is an effective growing medium when used with care and attention towards drainage and applying just the right amount of fertilizer.

Sandy Soil: Sandy soil is a type of loam soil composed of larger particles that are sand-sized or larger. This soil type has several benefits, particularly for those hoping to grow fruits in their gardens.

Its light texture allows for plenty of aeration, and the sandy soil's low moisture retention means gardeners don't have to worry about over-watering plants or dealing with clay-like mud.

Along with these benefits come some associated disadvantages. Sandy soil drains quickly and therefore doesn't contain as many nutrients essential for robust fruit growth, like nitrogen, potassium, phosphorus, etc.

Gardeners must make sure to supplement their sandy soil with organic matter or fertilizer to compensate for its nutrient deficiencies. Overall, sandy soil provides excellent aeration but requires supplementation if used for fruit gardening.

Chalk Soil: Chalk soil is a type of soil that is composed of clay, sand, and minerals. It has an alkaline pH level and neutral soil content and doesn't retain water or contain much organic matter.

The main benefit of using chalk soil in fruit gardening is its ability to provide good drainage; however, because it lacks organic matter, plants grown in this type of soil may need extra fertilizers added to promote vigorous growth.

Additionally, chalk soil can be heavy and unstable when wet, which makes it difficult to keep well-tilled if the garden location experiences heavy rains. Despite these challenges, with proper care and maintenance, a fruit garden using this type of soil can still yield lots of delicious, ripe fruits.

Loam Soil: Loam soil is renowned in gardening circles as the perfect balance of nutrients and minerals for crop cultivation. It is made up of a balanced combination of clay, sand, and organic matter, which makes it rich in nutrients and provides great drainage capabilities.

The benefit is that Loam soil can provide added fertility to plants without risking too much water retention or compaction. This type of soil will promote excellent plant growth, and nearly all fruit, such as apples and oranges, respond well when grown in this type of soil.

However, the disadvantage of using Loam soil for fruit trees is its susceptibility to over-saturating or drying out. Therefore success at cultivating high-yielding fruit crops depends on diligently managing the moisture levels near the root zone of each tree for optimal results.

SIGNS OF FERTILE AND HIGH-QUALITY SOIL

A healthy garden starts with healthy soil, but it can be difficult to tell if your patch has what it takes to grow nutritious fruit plants. As expected, you may have a few questions, and rightly so - curious to understand if your soil is healthy or not, so in the following we'll cover and identify essential characteristics of fertile garden soil. Now that we know why good soil matters, it's time to figure out what type you have.

What is Fertile Soil?

Fertile fruit garden soil is an ideal combination of nutri-ents, minerals, and pH for growing fruits and vegetables in a garden. It is made up of organic matter such as compost, manure, and leaves that provide essential macro and micro-nutrients like potassium and magnesium needed for successful crop growth.

Fertile fruit garden soil also requires careful attention to pH balance; different plants have different ideal acidity levels, so regular testing can ensure maximum productivity.

Proper fertility combined with adequate amounts of water will give you the best chance of harvesting hardy, healthy produce.

Fertile soil for fruit gardening has the following characteristics:

- Fertile soil for fruit gardening should be light in texture, well-drained, high in organic content, and slightly acidic to neutral.
- It has a high water retention capacity, which helps prevent damage from temperature extremes or droughts.
- Good tilth or structure is just as important in allowing oxygen and water penetration while providing support for growing plants.
- The right balance of essential nutrients, such as nitrogen, phosphorous, and potassium
- Fertile soil should provide drainage for water around the plant's roots to ensure they are not overwatered.
- It's free of debris and pollution, such as stone and plastic.
- It's rich in organic matter, such as compost or aged manure. Organic matter provides nutrients to plants. When a garden is rich in these resources, the soil will provide nutrients for the plants to grow, which means artificial fertilizers are often unnecessary.

- Its well-aerated soil allows air circulation and avoids the consequences of compaction.

THE ART OF CRAFTING PERFECT SOIL

Step 1: Test Your Soil

For an optimal and healthy garden, it is essential to understand the composition of your garden soil. Testing your garden soil can provide important information about its texture and chemical makeup, including levels of nutrients such as nitrogen, phosphorus, and potassium.

With this data, you can better develop enriching environments for your plants and diagnose issues such as improper pH balance or contamination from metals and poisons. Fortunately, testing your garden soil isn't difficult – as there are several methods for testing.

There's over-the-counter kits to explore soil pH levels, laboratory reports which include a broad spectrum of chemical elements used in soil analysis and home tests that measure the plant-available macro and micro-nutrients in the soil.

With a little effort upfront, you'll be equipped to identify what you need to add (or avoid) to create ideal conditions for long-term growth. Knowing this information can help ensure that you are nurturing an optimal environment for all of your plants.

Step 2: Clean Your Soil

Keeping your garden soil clean is a vital part of keeping your plants growing and thriving. Clean soil gets rid of any bacteria that can be harmful to your vegetation and allows the plants to access healthy amounts of oxygen and water.

The best way to keep your soil clean is by removing weeds, old vegetation, or debris. Composting is also a great option for gardeners looking for helpful ways to keep their soil clean; composted organic material will add essential minerals and nutrients back into the dirt.

Additionally, cover crops are another excellent way to ease the process of cleaning up debris from the soil while also helping keep weed seeds at bay. Taking time to care for your garden soil will benefit not only yourself but your plants too.

Step 3: Remove Infestations

Gardeners must pay close attention to their soil in order to identify any infestations before it escalates into a major issue. Penetrating your soil with the help of a spade and ensuring that you observe the roots of the plants is critical to catching infestations earlier.

Some signs of infestations include clumps of old, decayed egg masses or caterpillars on leaves, ants in the soil, or even moldy spots on organic matter lying on top of the soil.

If identified, it is crucial to remove infestations from garden soil as soon as possible, as they can cause long-term damage to your garden by creating nematodes or killing beneficial insects.

It is best to use natural methods such as introducing beneficial predators such as ladybugs into the affected area, which will naturally eradicate the pests. Natural remedies are preferred over chemicals to maintain healthy soil for future growth and fertility.

Remember not to remove all insects as some can benefit your garden and are necessary to its natural ecosystem. Not everything poses a threat. Some insects, such as bees, ladybirds, and ants, are beneficial to your garden, but others, such as cabbage worms, mites, and carrot rust flies, should be kept out of your garden.

Step 4: Treat Your Soil

The condition of your garden soil and how you treat it will have a major impact on the type and quality of plants that can be grown in it. Therefore, once you understand the conditions of your garden soil, it is important to take the necessary steps to ensure a healthy and fertile growing environment.

There are many different ways to do this, including adding organic matter such as compost or manure, checking and adjusting pH levels, testing for nutrient deficiencies, mulching, and aerating.

Treating the soil helps ensure plants receive all the essential nutrients they need giving them more vitality so they can better fend off disease and thrive in their growing environment.

Gardeners that give their gardens special treatment can look forward to enjoying an abundant harvest of healthy plants while using fewer resources in terms of fertilizer and water.

STORE-BOUGHT VS HOMEMADE SOIL TREATMENT

Gardening is a great way to enjoy the outdoors and grow your own edible goods. With many products available at local stores, there has never been an easier time for aspiring gardeners to get started.

On the other hand, experienced gardeners who are looking for more of a challenge may prefer preparing their own soil treatments from natural ingredients. Whether you buy already-made products or prepare something yourself, each option offers its own benefits and disadvantages that should be thoughtfully considered before taking the plunge.

No matter which approach you choose, the reward of having bountiful fruit plants will be worth it.

Homemade Soil Treatment

Gardeners understand the importance of nourishing their plants with healthy soil, so many choose to make their own homemade soil treatments for a cost-effective and customized method of support.

Not only do homemade soil treatments give gardeners control over the ingredients used to care for their plants, but they may also be potentially more efficient. Gardeners who combine organic matter like compost and proficiently balanced additives like fungicides can guarantee that the specific needs of their garden soil are being addressed.

Furthermore, homemade treatments provide an opportunity for gardeners to experiment with various recipes to see which offers the best results, meanwhile reducing waste by using an assortment of sustainable ingredients readily available.

In sum, there is a wide array of benefits that come from using homemade soil treatments instead of store-bought products.

Advantages of Homemade Soil Treatment

- Homemade soil treatments are a cost-effective and natural way to rejuvenate garden soil.
- They can improve the physical, chemical, and biological properties of soil, which results in healthier plants.
- You have the power to confidently know precisely how much nourishment your plants will receive - no more having to guess or hope that what you're giving them is enough.

Disadvantages of Homemade Soil Treatment

- Homemade soil treatments often require more time, energy, and effort than store-purchased treatments to produce the desired results.
- It can be challenging for gardeners to accurately measure the ingredients for DIY concoctions or to determine how long a certain mixture can be safely applied or stored. Extra testing for your homemade treatments may be necessary in some cases.
- Poor-quality ingredients from unreliable sources may lead to an imbalance in soil nutrition that could adversely affect plant growth.

- It requires work on your part, such as constant maintenance and upkeep of the conditions of your treatments.

Store-Bought Soil Treatment

Gardeners worldwide recognize the importance of soil, which is why many take the extra step of adding soil treatments to their gardens. Store-bought soil treatments are increasingly popular for multiple reasons.

It contains a blend of organic matter like compost or peat moss that helps improve drainage, nutrient uptake, and moisture retention in the soil. Additionally, store-bought soil treatments are often enriched with other elements such as gypsum, calcium carbonate, and iron to increase the fertility of the soil.

Store-bought treatments usually come in concentrated form, so only a small amount needs to be added in order to reap its benefits. Furthermore, store-bought soil treatments are typically tailored for specific types of plants.

They can provide them with specific nutrients or protection from pests or diseases that may otherwise harm them. Soil treatment is an integral part of gardening, and buying it at a store gives gardeners another tool for achieving a successful harvests.

Advantages of Store-Bought Soil Treatment

- Store-bought soil treatments create consistent results in terms of the desired nourishment that are often difficult to achieve with manual methods.

- Store-bought soil treatment is generally easier on people's budgets than other forms of garden care, and each use can last up to twice as long due to its concentrated nature.
- Store-bought treatments often have added benefits such as protection from pests, weeds, and disease management, helping gardeners avoid costly problems that can arise when gardening without the aid of quality treatment.
- Store-bought soil treatment can save time and effort. Gardeners don't need to spend hours preparing their soil manually.
- You don't have to wait months for treatment to mature before you use it.

Disadvantages of Store-Bought Soil Treatment

- Compared to homemade treatments, store-bought ones can be more costly when maintaining your garden.
- Many store-bought products contain chemicals that may harm beneficial insects or unintentionally upset the natural balance of the soil.

DECIDING WHAT FRUITS TO GROW

Growing your own fruits can be a satisfying and enjoyable experience, but with so many fruits to choose from, it might be difficult to determine what you should plant in your garden. Getting clear on your reasons for growing fruits can help you to determine the best types of fruit to cultivate.

Having a conscious approach enables strategic decisions when it comes to selecting products that will truly benefit your lifestyle and gardening goals. Oranges may be one of your family's favorite fruits to eat, or the thought and taste of homemade orange juice trumps store-bought on any given day; then choosing to grow those would be a perfect addition to your crops.

Is this the year you want to take your personal health to the next level? Then adding berries to your crops would be an excellent addition. For starters, berries are not only a delicious treat, but they are also incredibly nutritious.

Their high levels of antioxidants can reduce inflammation and the risk of certain diseases, while the flavonoids contained within them have been linked to improved brain function. Furthermore, the vitamins and minerals contained in them impact heart health in a positive manner by strengthening blood vessels and reducing cholesterol. With these reasons in mind, it's clear that berry consumption is beneficial for overall health and well-being.

You might be concerned about the quality of the grapes you buy from a local store and are looking for a better alternative. Growing your own grapes allows you to control what goes into them. By using organic growing techniques combined with pest-resistant varieties, one can avoid using unhealthy chemicals found in commercially grown produce.

The size of your garden is also a major factor in what kind of fruits you choose to grow. If you have a large plot of land to dedicate to gardening, you can take advantage of that space by planting trees to cultivate apples, pears, peaches, and more.

If your garden is smaller in size, then you could look into raising berries and other small fruits, such as plums or cherries, that don't need as much room for the roots. To get the most out of any size plot, make sure you pick appropriate varieties for the climate and regional conditions. This way, you can maximize the yield of whichever fruits you choose to grow and enjoy delicious harvests.

Finally, understanding your soil type is one of the most important steps when deciding what types of fruit to grow in your garden.

Not all fruits require the same type of soil to grow correctly, so if you want to get the most out of your harvest, you must research what type of soil and nutrients are best for the fruits you are planting.

Different kinds of soil can provide varying levels of minerals, nitrogen, and water retention. If fruit roots don't have access to these elements, then it won't receive all the necessary nutrition that it needs to blossom into a healthy plant with optimal yields.

If you attempt to grow a fruit plant that needs an alkaline environment in an acidic environment, chances are it won't grow properly. This may feel like your garden endeavors are wasted when the problem is that the plant is in the wrong soil conditions.

Growing nutritious fruits is always the end goal, so understanding the specific characteristics within your soil can be the key to success.

PLANTING & SOWING SEEDS: SOW FAR, SOW GOOD

Planting and sowing methods have a huge impact on the success of a garden. It can be daunting for beginner gardeners to understand the ins and outs of each planting and sowing method - from broadcasting to transplanting and drilling - it's important to take time to understand the difference.

Knowing the differences between each method makes you better equipped as a gardener; you can decide which crops can benefit most from planting versus sowing and which strategies will help provide optimal conditions for your plants.

Choosing the right method will not only increase the success of your garden but will also save you time and money in the long run. Knowing when to sow seeds, how deep to plant them, and what type of soil needs to be used are all key factors that can help your garden flourish.

Additionally, specific planting and sowing methods enable gardeners to group compatible species together so that there are fewer problems with disease issues amongst the various types of fruit. Ultimately, taking an informed approach can ensure that your hard work pays off in healthy, beautiful vegetation.

Below are some insightful and effective sowing techniques for planting. Some may be useful in the type of garden you want, and some may not, but it's always good to know various techniques.

You never know when you might want to change things up and grow something different or expand your garden to accommodate more fruits.

SOWING TECHNIQUES

Broadcasting

The broadcasting sowing method is a common practice used in agriculture to distribute seeds across a field. This method involves casting or throwing out the seed over an area of land without much regard for where each seed lands.

It is an effective way to spread crops like wheat and other grains, as well as vegetables, strawberries, or grass seeds. Generally, it is used when uniform dispersion is not necessary and can be performed quickly by hand, but can also be done mechanically with a drill or planter attachment.

This technique works best when there is enough soil moisture to sustain active germination, as broadcasted seeds need to come into contact with a moist environment to be properly fertilized and grow successfully.

Advantages

- It improves the speed of planting and makes sure seeds are spread out evenly in a relatively short amount of time.
- It gives gardeners the ability to make sure their seed lands evenly, with no gaps between the rows and no overlap.
- It can be used for container or raised bed gardens, as well.

Disadvantage

- It can result in inconsistencies with planted depths, thus making it more difficult to achieve uniform germination.
- Because seedlings are scattered instead of being placed intentionally in each space, weeds have a much higher chance of becoming part of the field.
- It's only suitable for seeds that don't need a specific amount of space to grow.
- It's only suitable for shallow-rooted plants.
- Broadcasting can lead to low yield due to incorrect seed density or over-competition between seeds for soil nutrients and water.

Dibbling

The Dibbling sowing method is a simple and effective way to prep a field for planting. It is an incredibly labor-efficient way of evenly distributing seed into an area with minimal effort.

The process involves using a handheld tool, known as a dibbler, to make small slits in the surface soil and dropping one or two seeds into each slit. Once completed, the soil can be covered by a light rake, and any excess removed.

This type of sowing is particularly useful when planting crops with large seeds, as it allows for a higher concentration of viable plants per given area compared to conventional broadcasting methods, which may generate overcrowding and reduced yields due to competition for resources.

Advantage

- This manual process provides the ability to build and customize spacing based on each crop's specific need.
- It can be done in all types of gardens.
- It's very organized and accurate.

Disadvantages

- This method of sowing can be particularly labor-intensive and time-consuming, which in turn could result in added costs for growers.

Drilling

The drilling-sowing method of planting is a frequent agricultural practice that involves the use of special machinery, typically a seeder, to place seeds directly into the soil.

This approach creates neat rows, which helps avoid weeds and promotes better nutrient absorption than if seeds were thrown onto the ground. Crops planted using this technique also receive more uniform water distribution, and pests can be held at bay due to the precise placement of seeds.

Drilling sowing is responsible for many successful harvests and has been used widely throughout Europe since the Middle Ages.

Advantages

- It helps to reduce the operating time and cost associated with planting seeds in the fields.

- Farmers that utilize this method can also expect higher grain yields than those who choose other sowing methods.
- Since this technique facilitates uniform depth sowing, it ensures better soil-seed contact and, therefore, accurate germination of seeds.
- The increased efficiency, speed, and accuracy of the seeding process allows more seeds to be planted on less land.
- This method enables quick germination since the seed is placed at the correct soil depth and can enable faster weed control due to a tighter canopy, thus reducing weeds around the plants.

Disadvantages

- This method requires more advanced machinery and thus increases costs.
- When it comes to operating such machinery, the farmer needs to have proper knowledge and skills, or else crops can suffer due to incorrect depth of seed placement or avoidable human errors.
- It can be time-consuming, especially when using a handheld drill.

Plough Sowing

The plow-sowing method is an effective and efficient way of seed placement. It enables farmers to distribute the seeds uniformly across their plots, helping ensure that all the plants receive the same amount of light, water, and nutrients.

The process involves plowing a furrow through the soil into which the seed is placed, followed by closing the furrow with a wheeled implement. This method allows for more precise spacing of plants, resulting in greater crop yields.

Currently, this type of sowing method is most common among large-scale farmers whose landholdings are too big for harvesting by hand. It is an age-old form of farming that has its roots in many ancient civilizations, but with advancements in modern machinery, it has become even easier and quicker for today's farmers to use this efficient approach to planting their crops.

Advantages

- In regard to soil composition, this kind of sowing can create an ideal environment for loosening soil particles and enriching them with oxygen.
- It's great for large, traditional in-ground gardens.
- It can be less costly when cattle are used.
- It's a fast way to sow seeds.

Disadvantage

- It can be expensive, especially with plow machines.

- Seeds can become overcrowded.

Transplanting

The transplanting sowing method is one of the most popular gardening methods for growing plants. It involves digging holes in the ground and then filling them up with already-sprouted seedlings or small plants.

This allows gardeners to get more precise spacing between plants, helps avoid overcrowding, and makes it easier to tend to each plant individually.

With transplanting sowing, you can start your garden months ahead of direct sowing, as you don't have to wait for seeds to sprout. It also offers more flexibility regarding how many plants of a particular variety you want to put in an area because you can space them accordingly depending on their size when transplanted.

Finally, it's also helpful if certain varieties don't do well in your region due to weather conditions or soil quality. By transplanting them in prepared beds at the right time of year, you may get good yields even in unfavorable conditions climates.

Advantages

- This method allows gardeners to save time and labor because they can sow the seeds indoors in a nursery, which minimizes the amount of weeds that have to be committed out manually.
- Nurseries can also provide controlled environments so plants can grow optimally before

transferring them to their designated locations in the field.

Disadvantages

- Transplanting sowing creates disruption between root systems during transferral, which makes them vulnerable; this increases the risk of associated diseases affecting the overall crop quality.
- Not all plants may survive.

READY, SET, GROW

Now that you know how to sow your fruit seeds, you have officially started your exciting gardening journey. Planting a fruit garden may seem like an enormous task, but the rewards are tremendous.

Properly caring for your garden is essential in order to reap the potential from every seed planted. To ensure success, it's essential to pay close attention to your garden. This includes monitoring irrigation, ensuring appropriate amounts of fertilizer, and pruning at the right times.

As you tend to your garden daily, be sure to also observe any changes that occur, such as new growth or any signs of disease or insects. If detected early, these issues can often be quickly treated. Additionally, staying patient and consistent with your gardening efforts can significantly improve harvests and production.

In order to create an environment where fruits can grow and flourish, proper care should be taken each season while keeping an eye on changes in temperature and climate conditions.

Your fruit garden soil is the very foundation of your plants. Paying close attention to the nutrition in your garden's soil is paramount if you are to produce high-quality, delicious fruits.

Without adequate nutrients and macronutrients in the right balance, many plants will not thrive or may even suffer fungal disease due to poor growing conditions. If you plan on fertilizing, it is essential to adjust the quantity based on what types of fruits you are trying to grow and any previous surveys of your soil's nutrient content.

Also, be sure to assess any compaction or poor quality of soil in your fruit garden by testing for proper acidity, drainage, and texture. It is also worth noting that paying close attention to the soil's moisture levels is equally important for promoting healthy fruiting in plants, so regular watering will be necessary all season long.

With attentive care and persistence, you can see your fruit gardens produce amazing results that come with great satisfaction.

CHAPTER 2
GROWING YOUR SUMMER RASPBERRIES

There's something special about growing your own fruit in the summer months, and raspberries are no exception. Not only are they a delicious treat to eat - either fresh or cooked into desserts, but raspberry bushes also provide beauty to your garden that can be enjoyed all summer.

Raspberries require little maintenance and will produce a significant harvest when grown in conditions that suit them well. In addition, growing your own raspberries allows you to experiment with different varieties and determine which are best for your climate and soil type - something you would not be able to do with pre-packaged store-bought berries.

Growing your own raspberries gives you the peace of mind that comes with knowing exactly where your food is coming from—no chemicals or air miles necessary.

THE RIGHT SOIL FOR RASPBERRIES

Knowing what type of soil to grow raspberries in can be the difference between success and failure in the garden. The ideal soil for raspberries during the summer months is one that's moist, has good drainage, and contains a balance of organic matter.

Sandy loam soils with pH levels between 5.5 and 7 are preferable due to their ability to retain water for extended periods without becoming flooded.

Because plants thrive and produce better when their needs are specifically catered to, it's important to have the right type of soil and other environmental elements around them - like sun, rain, and plenty of airflow. This allows for the absorption of nutrients they need while avoiding damage from pests or excess moisture.

Adding compost or mulch also helps encourage healthy growth by maintaining adequate moisture levels and creating an environment where nutrients are readily available. Understanding the characteristics of the ideal soil will enable you to alter your existing soil, ensuring your raspberry plants have the best chance of producing healthy, vibrant, and delicious raspberries.

So be sure to test your existing soil. Vital information such as the current pH level, nutrient composition, and drainage is the type of data required to ensure your raspberries are being grown in a hospitable environment.

Raspberries Plant Diseases

Plant diseases can be a significant problem for raspberry gardeners, as disease-ridden plants produce far less fruit than healthy plants. Common causes of disease include fungi, bacteria, and viruses. Fungal diseases are often caused by excess moisture.

To prevent them, gardeners should avoid overwatering their plants and make sure the soil is well-drained. Bacterial diseases can be hard to identify and are typically found on the older parts of the plant - they can be treated with fungicides or bactericides.

Temperature fluctuations can also contribute to disease development in raspberries, as plants struggle to adapt to unusually heavy rainfall, frosty temperatures or days with extreme heat. Poor maintenance practices, such as incorrect irrigation and pruning techniques, can also leave plants vulnerable to fungi and other pathogens.

Raspberries are commonly affected by a range of diseases, each with its own particular characteristics and treatments.

Powdery mildew is one example, characterized by gray or white patches on the leaves and stems of the plant that take on the appearance of flour. This disease can be prevented with proper spacing between plants, avoiding overhead watering, selecting resistant varieties, and minimizing fertilization.

Anthracnose is another issue affecting raspberries, resulting in brown spots on the leaves, which usually diminish during hot weather. The best mechanisms for prevention are avoiding overhead irrigation in the late evening as wetness will incubate this disease, along with removing affected leaves from the raspberry bush promptly to stop infestations from spreading to healthy parts of the plant.

Others include root rot, leaf spot, and Verticillium wilt. These diseases can cause leaves to discolor and curl, rot on the leaves and canes of the plants, which can lead to limited fruiting.

In order to prevent these diseases from affecting raspberry plants, it's important to practice good farming methods such as fertilizing adequately, controlling pests, rotating crops, cleaning up around plants after harvesting season, providing good soil/garden drainage, and using resistant varieties when available.

When growing raspberries, it is important to be aware of the types of plants you in the same area. Planting vegetables like potatoes, eggplants, and tomatoes near raspberry canes can promote various diseases and problems with their growth.

Additionally, certain plants, such as sweet peas and beans, may cause competition for resources like water and sunlight, so it's best to avoid these as well. You also want to prevent weeds by keeping your raspberry patch well-weeded and mulched regularly.

Finally, try to place your raspberry plants far away from shrubs or trees with similar pest problems as the berry bush since they will likely draw the same bugs and predators.

With that being said, there are several fruits that make great companion plants for the raspberry bushes. Examples of friendly companions include blueberries, blackberries, and currants. Other hardy fruits like apples and pears also provide a good environment to support a raspberry patch.

Planting marigolds among these fruit-bearing bushes can help ward off pests and grow healthier crops at harvest time. Additionally, many herbs make great neighbors for raspberries, including rosemary, fennel, thyme, oregano, sage, and even chamomile. All these options make raspberries a great addition, no matter what climate you live in.

HOW TO SOW RASPBERRIES

Correct Season to Sow Raspberries

It's important to note that the timing of when to grow raspberries will depend on your region and local climate. Generally, it's best to plant raspberry plants in late Autumn or early Winter, around the same time bare-root trees are planted.

When planting raspberries outdoors, be sure to choose an area with good drainage and nearby sunlight. Autumn provides the perfect conditions for raspberry bushes - the combination of sunlight and warmer days helps the fruit mature to its sweetest flavor, while cooler nights allow for a more abundant yield.

In addition, planting new canes during this season ensures plenty of space and nutrients when it comes time to harvest them in summer. With an optimal climate and plenty of resources, you can rest assured that growing raspberries come autumn will result in delectable fruits.

Plant Needs and Requirements

Growing your own raspberries from seed is an economical way of having your own berry patch - plus, it can be very rewarding and fun. Germinating the raspberry seeds is a simple process that requires no special equipment or green-thumb expertise.

Armed with a packet of fresh raspberry seeds, you can easily provide yourself with an abundant supply of nutritious fruit for many years to come. Additionally, you can customize your plantings to suit individual tastes, such as trying out different varieties of raspberries and selecting those that best fit your climate, pest resistance, or other desired qualities.

With just a few small steps when planting raspberry seeds, you can start on the path to enjoying a bounty of bright and juicy homegrown berries every season.

Growing raspberries indoors can be done with just a little bit of patience and supplies – so to get started, you'll need some raspberry seeds, a good potting soil mix, and containers with drainage holes.

First, soak your seeds in warm water overnight. This will help to break down the seed's hard coat and start the germination process.

Then prepare the soil and containers by mixing the potting soil with some sterile sand, filling the containers, and soaking them so they are moist but not drenched.

Next, plant four raspberry seeds in each container, spaced at least an inch apart, cover them lightly with soil, then mist gently with a spray bottle of water to help keep the seeds moist.

Place the seeded containers in an area away from direct sunlight where temperatures remain cool (60-65 degrees Fahrenheit) and regularly check for signs of germination - usually within two to three weeks.

Once the sprouts have begun to emerge, use indirect sunlight, such as filtered sunlight through a windowsill or grow light system, to encourage further growth.

Now that your seeds have started sprouting, this is an indication that soon they are due to be transplanted to their new and permanent environment. This can be in raised beds, containers placed on balconies and terraces, or for those with larger spaces available growing in the ground.

Raspberry seedlings should be transplanted when they reach four to five inches in height or have developed at least two sets of leaves. The best time of year to transplant raspberry seedlings is between late spring and early summer when the soil is both warm and moist.

At this stage, the soil should be loose enough and warm enough for them to handle a transplanting without too much shock. The soil should be well-nourished with compost or other organic matter before planting.

Also, remember that raspberries prefer slightly acidic soil. It's best to wait until all frost danger has passed since planting too early may expose your emerging plants to cold weather, potentially slowing their growth or killing them before they have a chance to bear fruit.

Spacing and Measurement

When it comes to growing raspberry seedlings, spacing and measurements are critical. Planting your raspberry seeds too close together will lead to competition for essential resources such as water and nutrients, while planting them too far apart will cause the plants to be weak and spindly.

The best way to ensure success with raspberry growth is by giving each seedling ample space without overcrowding the pot or bed. This means that larger pots are better than smaller ones, and a spacing of at least 4 inches between each raspberry seedling is advised for optimal growth.

Furthermore, care should be taken during transplantation so that roots do not become damaged or tangled, as this will hinder their ability to absorb vital resources from the soil. When given the proper conditions according to measurements and spacing guidelines, raspberries can flourish in any setting and provide sweet rewards for gardeners of all types.

MAINTAINING YOUR RASPBERRIES

Raspberries are the perfect addition to any home because they can survive both indoors and outdoors, making them incredibly versatile. However, maintaining them requires a bit of skill and knowledge. Proper watering, soil mixture, and sunlight are all critical components for successful growth.

Additionally, it's important to prune raspberry plants during their dormant season - this helps the plant maintain its shape and prevents hindrance during the summer months when the fruit is ripe for picking. With a bit of patience and guidance, growing raspberries can be a great hobby that will bring joy for years to come.

Pruning and Thinning Your Raspberries

Pruning and thinning your raspberry patch is essential for ensuring the optimal health of your plants. Thinning helps alleviate overcrowded raspberries, resulting in significantly increased airflow and reduced humidity, which restricts fungal growth.

Additionally, pruning encourages better production of fruits and yields as it improves air circulation and daylight penetration to lower branches. Pruned raspberry brambles also take up less space while providing more efficient access for weeding, fertilizing, harvesting, and pest control.

Lastly, timely pruning is paramount to preventing diseases like raspberry spur blight from spreading amongst new growth. By dedicating a relatively small amount of time to trimming your berries on an annual or bi-annually depending on the bush type, you are investing in the overall longevity and sustainability of your raspberry patch.

Raspberry bushes need to be pruned and thinned for the health of the bush, as well as the quality of their fruits. Fortunately, this is a relatively simple process that can be done with garden clippers or pruning shears.

The goal is to remove unhealthy canes and those that do not bear fruit while allowing the healthy ones to remain untouched. This will promote new growth and allow light and air to circulate through the shrub.

Thinning should also be done after blooming and early summer on any raspberry plants with too many fruits already growing. By removing some of these fruits, it allows other flowers to become pollinated more efficiently and for the remaining fruits to become bigger and juicier.

Watering Raspberries

When caring for your raspberry plants, one of the most important things to keep in check is the watering. It is essential that you water your raspberries deeply and regularly to ensure healthy fruits. The best time to water them is in the morning when temperatures are still cool. That way, the soil has plenty of time to absorb the moisture before it gets too hot and much of it evaporates.

During summer, your raspberry bushes may need to be watered up to nearly every day if there is no rain or humidity to prevent wilting or burning of their delicate leaves.

Depending on the climate and the variety of raspberry plants, raspberries require anywhere from 2 to 4 inches of water per week during the growing season to get adequate moisture in the soil - either from rainfall or supplemental irrigation.

Yet too much water can be just as detrimental as too little, so it's important to find a balance between giving your raspberries enough water and avoiding overly soggy soils that can cause root rot and other damages.

With careful management and care, you can ensure your raspberry plants have the water they need to thrive.

Fertilization For Raspberries

Fertilization is an incredibly important part of maintaining healthy raspberry fruit plants since it helps to ensure that the plants receive adequate amounts of the essential nutrients they need to produce abundant and delicious fruit.

Fertilizers help improve soil quality, boost soil fertility, increase crop yields, and make sure that raspberry plants get access to key nutrients such as nitrogen, phosphorus, and potassium. An added benefit of regular fertilization is that it encourages vigorous growth as well as erect branching, which aids in a higher level of airflow throughout your raspberry plant's foliage.

Taking good care of your raspberry plants with consistent fertilization will go a long way towards preventing common issues like poor drainage and stunted fruiting.

An all-purpose, well-balanced NPK fertilizer should provide your plants with the primary nutrients in a ratio of approximately 10-10-10. This will help keep them healthy over the course of their growing season and support good fruit production.

Additionally, many gardeners find that applying fish emulsion or a seaweed extract helps to stimulate lush foliage growth as well as fruit production. Fertilizer should be applied in springtime when the buds on the raspberry plants begin to swell.

Routine applications every three to four weeks throughout the growing season are ideal for ensuring optimal plant nutrition levels. Lastly, make sure you don't overdo it. Too much fertilizer can cause the burning of roots and other problems - start with small doses of fertilizer and add more over time to determine what amount works best for your raspberry patch.

Following the manufacturer's directions carefully is also a great way to ensure you aren't over-fertilizing, as high nitrogen levels can be catastrophic for your raspberry plants.

PROTECTING YOUR RASPBERRIES

Extreme Temperatures

Raspberries are a delicious and versatile fruit, perfect for snacks, desserts, and salads. However, because of their thin-skinned nature, these berries must be protected against heat, cold, wind, and rain. If they are exposed to intense heat or frost, the bushes can suffer extensive damage, and the fruits may not develop properly or taste right.

To limit this risk, plant raspberries in well-drained soil in a sunny yet sheltered area of your garden. Make sure you mulch around the base of the plant, as this helps to keep the soil temperature regulated. When very hot weather arrives, use shade cloths or other forms of lightweight fabric to cover your raspberry crops and shield them from direct sunlight. In cold weather, add an extra layer of protection with blankets, straw, or pine needles placed around the plants' crowns to stop chill winds from reaching them.

Additionally, you should choose varieties of raspberries that are suitable for your local climate - some may be more tolerant to extreme temperatures than others. Finally, location plays an important role, too - try planting raspberries in a sheltered spot, such as near a hedge or wall.

Taking these simple steps will help ensure that your raspberry plants continue to thrive even in the toughest weather conditions.

Protecting Raspberries From Pest

Protecting raspberries from pests is a challenge for gardeners, as the berries attract a variety of insects. Gardeners should take a comprehensive approach to protect raspberries, including learning about the local pests in the area and their lifecycles.

Pruning damaged stems and using row covers over plants can protect them from some pests while also providing warmth and moisture retention. Insect control strategies can also be used, such as introducing beneficial insects or using controlled sprays of natural products, such as bacillus thuringiensis (Bt), when necessary.

A daily inspection of potential predators like slugs and caterpillars should also become a necessary routine. The best way to do this is by checking the top and bottom of the foliage. Hand-picking the pests off plant leaves or a sharp spray of water can be an effective solution if there aren't too many to manage.

Foil collars placed at soil level around each bush are a great preventative measure against both grasshoppers and rodents.

HARVESTING RASPBERRIES

Growing raspberries can be a rewarding experience - with the right care and attention, you can harvest a delicious crop in as little as 18 months. The amount of time it takes to get your own raspberries depends on the variety you are growing. Some varieties, such as early-season varieties, have shorter harvesting times than later ones.

Other important factors include planting time, location, and length of the season. When properly taken care of, raspberries can produce fruit for several years - however, if you want to ensure continuous production in subsequent years, it is important to practice good management techniques like pruning and fertilizing.

Harvesting your own raspberries can be a fulfilling experience. Before you begin, inspect the plant's stems for signs of thorns. If wearing a pair of gardening gloves, use them when plucking the ripe berries - they should come off easily and in one piece.

When searching for mature fruits, it helps to know their color, ripe raspberries are typically red in color. Do not wait too long, though, as overripe berries will not have the same flavor.

It is easy to identify ripe raspberries when there is no white center present at the fruit's end. To harvest, use a gentle twisting motion and carefully pull them off the plant before placing them in a basket or container for transport.

For the best flavors, try and harvest on dry days during mid-morning when the fruit is at its peak ripeness. Once all the red fruits are picked from a stem, look to see if any green fruits have developed, as these are not yet ready to eat.

With a bit of effort using these tips and tricks, you'll be harvesting your own delicious raspberries in no time.

SAVING RASPBERRIES SEEDS

Raspberries are a tasty and nutritious snack that can be enjoyed in many different ways. Harvesting raspberry seeds is a great way to grow your own plants, ensuring top-quality fruit year after year.

It's fairly straightforward as well; simply wait until the raspberries on your bush have turned full red and ripe before harvesting them. Collect the ripe berries gently, pulling them directly from the vine with utmost care so you don't damage the vines.

Put them into a bowl and mash them up with your hands until they form a pulp-like mixture. Separate the pulp from the liquid by pouring it through a sieve, leaving only the seeds in the bottom of your bowl.

Once you have carefully separated all of the seeds from their pods, pour them out onto a piece of clean paper towel and spread them out evenly, allowing them to air dry overnight.

Once fully dried, store the seed in an airtight container or zip-lock bag, label it with the variety of berries and current dates, then place it in a cool dry place away from direct sunlight. Following these simple processes will ensure you successfully conserve your raspberry seeds for future use.

CHAPTER 3
GROWING YOUR SUMMER PEARS

G rowing your summer pears is a great way to enjoy nature and reap the benefits of harvesting bountiful produces. You get to experience the magical moments of tending to, nurturing, and caring for your plants, and you'll also be rewarded with an abundance of delicious, ripe, and juicy pears – perfect for pies, preserves, or just eating fresh from the tree.

You can choose from various varieties based on their flavor profile or growing conditions. Homegrown pears also provide environmentally friendly benefits like helping pollinators and minimizing food waste due to being picked perfectly ripe compared to store-bought fruit that often has to be picked prematurely for shipping.

Growing your own pears gives you control over every element, including where you source your seeds, how organic they can be, and even the climate they thrive in.

THE RIGHT SOIL FOR PEARS

One of the most important steps to take before cultivating your fruit garden is understanding the soil condition you are working with. Testing your soil can be incredibly beneficial in helping determine what plants will thrive and what nutritional needs it has.

Soil tests can tell you your land's pH levels, nutrient content, and salinity levels - this information allows gardeners to add or remove elements from their gardens as needed. In addition, soil testing helps guard against plant damage due to the overapplication of nutrients and other impacts from hidden contaminants that may be residing in the ground.

By taking the time to properly check and understand your soil composition before cultivating, you will find yourself more prepared for a more successful yield at harvest time.

Summer pears need the right soil to grow correctly - without the correct type of soil, a bountiful harvest will be hard to come by. Preparing the land for optimal growth of summer pears starts by understanding what type of soil is best for them.

Sandy loam soils are ideal for cultivating summer pears as they provide excellent drainage, air exposure, and nitrogen for robust growth. It's also important to adjust both pH levels and nutrient content according to the amount of organic matter found in the soil, as this varies from region to region.

Summer pears grow best in soil with a pH of 6.5 to 7.5. The soil should be rich, well-drained, and loamy, containing small amounts of organic matter so the pear tree can absorb the nutrients it needs for growth.

Furthermore, summer pears need plenty of sunlight and protection from extreme temperatures - a location that receives at least 6 hours of full sun light and can also provide shade is perfect for this variety of pear trees.

Pear Plant Diseases

Pear trees are a fantastic addition to any garden, providing sweet, juicy fruit. Unfortunately, they can also be prone to a variety of diseases and pests which can significantly reduce the crop yield or even kill the trees if left unchecked.

Common pear plant diseases include metarhizium anisopliae, scab, fire blight, and powdery mildew. To combat these diseases, it is best to properly identify and diagnose them to determine the best treatment strategies.

Removing diseased fruit or branches and applying fungicide sprays for rust and mildew will help mitigate against the spread of disease-causing organisms.

Furthermore, regular pruning of branches helps improve air circulation within the tree canopy, which decreases humidity levels within the plant, thus preventing fungal growth and spread.

Prevention methods such as adequate control of insects like aphids that transmit some pathogens should be implemented, as well as using strong cultivar varieties that are resistant to common diseases.

Additionally, proper sanitation should be practiced by removing dead leaves and improving soil drainage around trees so there isn't standing water where diseases can spread quickly. Proper watering practices with mulching of soil around plants will help maintain healthy root systems, which provide greater resistance against disease attacks.

To ensure your pear tree grows healthy, there are certain plants you should avoid planting around it. A common issue is root competition - pear trees require quite a bit of water which may draw these resources away from other nearby plants.

Competing root systems could also stress the tree as they fight for nutrition, potentially making it more vulnerable to disease and pests. Avoid planting large shrubs near it, such as lilacs or viburnums, or annuals and perennials like sunflowers and zinnias. If overly vigorous climbers such as roses, wisteria, or clematis are planted close by, be sure to prune them frequently so that their roots don't compete with your pear tree's.

However, some plants also provide great benefits for your pear trees, by simply planting them within close proximity - for starters, they can assist each other nutritionally.

For example, if you plant berry bushes around a pear tree, the nitrogen in the nitrogen-fixing berry roots will be available to help nourish the tree as it grows.

Apple trees are a great companion as they offer nutritionally similar fruits while providing nitrogen-rich soil thanks to their deep root systems. Quince trees are also a great choice, as they can thrive in many climates while needing little care and attention. Moreover, quinces produce pectin, which aids the ripening process of pears and other nearby fruits.

Apricot trees are another excellent choice given the multiple other benefits, such as increased antioxidant levels in nearby sunlight or shade-loving fruiting plants. Additionally, apricots produce fragrant flowers, creating an even more beautiful garden.

HOW TO SOW PEARS

Correct Season to Sow Pears

While pears can generally be grown in all seasons, most varieties need to be planted when the temperatures are mild - if planted in winter when it is too cold, pear trees will struggle to produce fruit.

There are three variables that need to be considered when deciding when to plant pear trees - the type of climate, the desired harvest date, and the variety you are trying to grow.

The best time to plant a pear tree is during the late winter or early spring months when temperatures stay above freezing but below 65 degrees Fahrenheit. During these months, rain and soil moisture is high and beneficial for the growing tree.

The best time to sow chosen pear tree varieties is from February to April in warmer climates and as late as May in colder regions. Planting pears in rich soil that drains well and allows for adequate moisture recovery between watering cycles is also essential. When planted in line with their needs, these beautiful and versatile trees can bear plentiful amounts of succulent fruit for years.

Plant Needs and Requirements

Growing pear trees from seed is a rewarding experience that requires patience and perseverance. The first step to success is to select a variety of pear trees that will suit your garden and your preferences. Once decided, seeds need to be obtained from reputable source as quality can vary significantly.

The next step is to allow the seeds to stratify and soften by exposing them to cold temperatures for around four weeks - this can be done by placing them in the refrigerator. After this period, planting in good potting soil is necessary.

Prepare individual pots with potting soil and plant the seeds at least an inch deep. Be sure to keep the planting area in a warm spot with plenty of indirect light, and make sure to keep it moist during the growing period.

Pear trees, like many other plants, rely on the germination of their seeds for growth and survival. However, the conditions for successful germination can be quite specific.

Many factors come into play, but one of the most crucial is temperature. In the case of pear seeds, the optimal temperature range for germination is between 65°F and 75°F. Anything below 55°F, the seeds may simply lie dormant, waiting for warmer weather to arrive.

Conversely, if it is too hot with temperatures above 80°F, the seeds could be damaged or even killed off before they have a chance to sprout. Understanding these temperature

requirements is essential for any gardener or fruit enthusiast looking to cultivate their own pear tree.

Once your little trees have sprouted and reached about six
inches tall, it's time to move them outdoors or into larger
raised beds . During transplanting, ensuring adequate
drainage for the plant's root system is vital and that soil
moisture does not become too extreme.

In addition, avoiding disturbing or damaging the delicate
root systems when transferring from one location to
another is an essential step for a successful transplant.
With some effort and care, your pear tree can grow strong,
healthy and produce delicious fruit.

Spacing and Measurement

It is essential to have correct spacing and measurements
when transplanting pear seedlings because it can significantly affect the quality of the fruit produced.

When seedlings are not given proper spacing, overcrowding can occur, which leads to a decrease in sunlight
absorption and an increase in competition for water and
nutrients. Without proper nutrition and enough space, the
trees cannot reach their full fruit-bearing potential.

Additionally, when seedlings are planted too close to one
another, their growth can become tangled, making it difficult for maintenance, such as pruning or pest control. To
ensure healthy development from the seedling stage to
fruit-bearing trees, growers must take the time to consider
desired tree sizes and create plans with accurate spacing
measurements before planting.

When planting pear seedlings, it is vital to give them plenty of breathing room - this is especially true for varieties of pear trees that require additional space for their larger spread, such as Bartlett or Bosc.

Spacing of between 15 and 20 feet should be reserved for all trees, regardless of the variety being planted. Of course, if space is limited, fruit trees can also be trained to grow up on a wall or fence where they're given less space.

Additionally, be sure to measure the depth of your planting hole correctly, as pears seedlings prefer to be planted 2-3 times deeper than they were originally growing. Allowing enough tree-to-soil contact helps ensure better root development, providing greater access to water and essential minerals while facilitating proper drainage.

Further considerations should be considered if pears are being heavily pruned or grown in containers. In any case, proper spatial measurements will ultimately result in healthier and more productive pear trees.

MAINTAINING YOUR PEARS

Maintaining your pear trees is essential not only for the beauty and fruit they provide but to ensure their long-term health. Taking the time to prune, fertilize, and control pests can help your pear trees look their best and reduce their disease susceptibility. Regular inspections are also essential for identifying potential problems before they worsen, thus preserving the integrity of your tree's structure over time. Investing time and money in regular maintenance will reap the rewards in both form and fruit.

Pruning and Thinning Your Pear Trees

Pruning and thinning your pear trees is an integral part of keeping them healthy. It helps promote strong growth, reduces disease, and prevents overcrowding.

By pruning the trees, you can encourage branches to grow in the desired direction and ensure light and air can reach the tree's interior. Thinning the fruit encourages larger, sweeter fruits by limiting competition among immature pears for pollination and nutrition from the soil.

Regular pruning and thinning of trees also help reduce pests that can damage foliage and fruit production. Making sure to perform these activities will ensure a healthy harvest for years to come.

That said, knowing when to prune your tree and how much to thin it is essential so you don't damage it or reduce the fruit yields. It can help create healthier plants that can handle heat, cold, disease, and pests better if done correctly.

When pruning, you must consider factors such as size, structure, and shape consistent with the variety you've decided to grow. The same goes for thinning. Depending on the type of pear tree you have, it will require either annual or every other year pruning and regular thinning to keep it healthy and productive.

To get started, make sure to have the right tools and equipment, including sharp pruners, loppers, and saws. Then, carefully assess your tree's branches, and remove any dead, damaged, or diseased ones.

Next, thin out the dense areas, leaving enough space between the branches and fruiting spurs. Lastly, remove any water sprouts or suckers that appear at the base of the tree. Finally, follow up regularly with inspection and additional pruning and thinning if necessary, to create an even canopy full of juicy, delicious pears.

By taking the time to correctly prune and thin your pear trees, you will be rewarded with abundant harvests of tasty fruit.

Watering Pears

Watering pears trees correctly is vital for a healthy harvest each season. If the tree does not receive enough water, it will struggle to provide adequate fruits due to insufficient hydration levels, which may lead to poor tasting and small fruits. Insufficient watering can also cause the premature dropping of fruits and leaves from the tree and also encourage the spread of disease or pest infestations in the area.

On the other hand, overwatering pears trees can result in root rot, which can be deadly for your trees if not treated properly. Therefore, providing just enough water to meet your pear tree's needs will ensure you get a delicious harvest every season.

Pear trees require careful and consistent watering to flourish, and watering them the right way is important. The best approach is to give your pear trees a deep soak twice weekly during summer and less often in winter.

When applying water, make sure to do so generously but also evenly - this will promote root growth in both directions from the trunk and improve moisture retention in the soil. It can also help prevent future problems with drought stress and pests.

Additionally, mulch the base of your pear tree with 3-4 inches of compost or wood chips, which can further promote healthier growth by retaining moisture and suppressing weed growth that might otherwise compete for nutrients with your precious pears.

Fertilization For Pears

Fertilization is one of the most important practices for pear fruit trees. Without adequate nutrients, pear trees cannot produce large, juicy fruits. Even if a tree can grow without fertilization, it will not bear fruit that is as well-developed or tasty. When a tree is correctly fertilized with the right amounts at proper intervals, its flowers and fruits can develop better.

The right type of fertilizer can also allow the soil to retain much-needed moisture so that the trees remain healthy and fruitful throughout the season.

Furthermore, adding organic matter like compost, manure, bone meal, and fish emulsion on top of the soil helps nourish it and create an ideal environment for strong roots to anchor the trees in place and promote better health overall.

Compost is a rich source of organic matter that helps improve the soil's structure, while manure provides nitrogen and other essential nutrients. Bone meal is a slow-release fertilizer rich in phosphorus, which is essential for root development, while fish emulsion is an excellent source of nitrogen and other trace elements.

Additionally, fertilizing pear trees helps increase the root zone's microbial activity to better process essential substances like nitrogen, phosphorus, and potassium, all of which are necessary components of strong and hardy plants.

Sufficient fertilizer also allows the tree to resist diseases and compensate for any imbalances or deficiencies caused by weather changes. Ultimately, an adequately fertilized fruit tree provides sumptuous fruits and serves as a source of resilience against taxing conditions.

Fertilizers are an essential part of the growth and maintenance of any pear tree. However, not all fertilizers are alike, so it's essential to consider which is best for your pear tree. The type and timing of fertilizer you use depends on the age of the plant - young pear trees will require more frequent, smaller applications, whereas older trees should be fed just once a year.

While organic fertilizers are generally regarded as more beneficial for the soil and the environment, synthetic fertilizers may be necessary if your soil is very low in certain essentials like phosphorous and potassium.

Generally, when applying the fertilizer, look for a balanced three-part nitrogen-phosphate-potassium (NPK) ratio, such as 10-10-10, or specific nutrients reliant on the type of pear tree you have.

Once you've selected an appropriate fertilizer, make sure to apply it at least once a season, particularly during peak growing times such as late spring and early summer, while keeping in mind that too much of any fertilizer can have a negative effect on the root system of your pear trees.

PROTECTING YOUR PEAR TREES

Extreme Temperatures

One of the main ways to ensure your pear trees don't suffer in extreme temperatures is to plant them in a shaded area with good drainage. This will help shield them from more extreme temperatures and reduce their risk of suffering root rot or disease due to standing water.

During hot weather, keeping your tree well-watered and mulched is crucial. This will help regulate the temperature around the roots and keep them cool. If you want an extra layer of protection for young or newly planted trees, you can build a "trellis" or provide some other shading. This will also help block direct sunlight from hitting them on scorching days and prevent winds from disturbing their delicate roots.

In cold winter months, you should wrap the trunks with tree wraps to protect them from freezing temperatures, which can damage delicate bark and slow down growth.

Additionally, pruning weak branches helps prevent damage from high winds that often come in winter months. With a few simple precautions like these, you can ensure your pear fruit trees are strong and healthy all year round.

Protecting Pears From Pest

When it comes to protecting pear trees from pests, prevention is always the best course of action. To safeguard their pear trees, gardeners should start by taking preventative measures such as keeping weeds away from the tree root area, cleaning up fallen leaves and fruits, and keeping good airflow around the trunk. Pruning off any dead or dying branches can also help reduce pest infestations.

Planting pest-resistant pear tree varieties, such as the Magness pear, and regularly checking your trees for signs of infestation can also help protect them. For example, look into your tree's canopy and inspect the leaves for symptoms such as black spots or discoloration caused by insects like aphids.

Taking other steps like encouraging beneficial insects like ladybugs and pollinator-friendly flowers or trapping pesky critters in sticky traps are more effective ways to protect your fruit trees from potential pests.

Finally, it may be necessary to use chemicals approved for organic agriculture to keep serious pest problems under control. With the right combination of preventive measures and targeted treatments, gardeners can keep their pear fruit tree healthy all year.

HARVESTING PEARS

Pear fruit trees take anywhere from 3 to 8 years before the first harvest is ready to be picked. Depending on the type of pear tree, it may require patience before a bountiful crop is available to harvest each year.

After the initial 3-8 year period, pear trees typically bear fruit every spring and summer months until winter arrives. If you have a large collection of pear trees, there are some different cultivation techniques you can use to ensure that your harvests are plentiful and evenly distributed throughout the year.

It is important to prune carefully throughout the growing period to aid good structure and support healthy growth and flowering. With proper nutrition, plants should begin bearing at the end of their fourth season, but commercial growers often wait until they are six or seven years old to achieve greater yields.

Harvesting pears from fruit trees can be an exciting and rewarding experience. The key to a successful harvest is timing - depending on the variety of pear trees, ripe fruit is ready for picking between late summer and early fall when it has changed color and can easily be pulled away from the branch.

You can also check the pears are ripe by lightly squeezing them. To ensure that you don't miss a single pear, weekly inspections are necessary so that you may note any changes in color or texture.

As soon as your fruit is ready, harvest it quickly and carefully with pruning shears, leaving a couple of inches of stem attached to the fruit before storing it. You can also use a ladder to reach the higher branches and grasp the fruit firmly between your thumb and forefinger.

Gently pull the pears off until they give way in your hand – there's no need to yank or pull hard, as this can damage both the tree and the fruit. Once harvested, bring the pears indoors right away so they don't spoil. With some patience and proper timing, growers can enjoy success harvesting their very own pear trees.

SAVING PEAR SEEDS

Harvesting pear fruit seeds is a great way to save money when you want to start a new garden. By collecting your pear fruit seeds and germinating them, you can easily recreate the same type of tree.

Before harvesting, it's best to choose fruit that is fully ripe on the tree. Once picked, carefully cut the fruits in half and remove all the seeds - be sure to immediately spread them out so they do not become moldy. Then place them on a clean surface with newspaper and allow them to dry completely.

Once dry, store the seeds in an airtight container in a cool, dry place with low humidity. Ensure they are adequately labeled so you don't forget which variety they are.

With these simple steps, you can ensure your pear tree seeds are stored safely and ready for planting whenever you're ready.

CHAPTER 4
GROWING YOUR SUMMER APPLES

Apples are one of the most versatile fruits, perfect for baking pies and adding that crunch to any fruit salad. Instead of heading to your local grocery store for summer apples, why not try growing your own.

Growing your own apples in the summer is not only fun and rewarding but provides ripe fruit without all of the additives that come from store-bought variations.

You can pick fresh apples from your garden directly into the pie dish and enjoy juicy apples just plucked off the tree – no added sugar or preservatives necessary. Not to mention, homegrown apples provide an environmentally friendly option when choosing what type of fruit to harvest.

Cultivating your own apples can also provide an excellent opportunity for exercise, encouraging you to get out in the sun and enjoy the outdoors.

Along with the physical benefits, growing your own apples can also help you save money on produce and provide reassurance that what you are eating is organic and free of any unwanted chemicals or materials.

There is something special about picking fruit straight from a tree that makes it feel even sweeter than buying it at the store. Whether alone or with friends and family, growing your apples is worth considering this summer.

THE RIGHT SOIL FOR APPLES

When considering starting an apple orchard, one of the most important steps is ensuring that your soil is conducive to growing such trees. By testing your soil beforehand, you can ensure nutrient levels and appropriate pH balance are in range.

Testing will help identify what types of fertilizers and other treatments are necessary for growing healthy apple trees that produce a good yield. Not having the appropriate nutrients in your soil can lead to stunted growth or even cause your trees to die, so investing in a soil test before starting a new orchard can save you time and money down the road.

Knowing what type of soil you have ensures that all the other factors involved with creating an affordable and bountiful apple orchard will be successful.

Apples need soil with good drainage, so a medium texture is ideal - sandy loam soils are best. It should have some sand to loosen the soil and plenty of organic material to hold moisture.

A pH level between 6.0 and 7.5 is best to ensure the right balance of nutrients for the growing trees throughout the summer season. Testing kits are available to help you accurately determine your soil's composition and adjust accordingly, if necessary with additions such as lime or compost.

Clay soils should be avoided, as they generally don't allow for proper drainage and may cause your apple trees to struggle during hot weather. When planting your trees, enrich the soil with aged manure or compost, and make sure you maintain adequate irrigation during hot days.

Maintaining a healthy balance of air and water in the root zone for at least three feet below the surface is optimal for apple tree growth and production. With patience, proper soil preparation will help you reap generous crops of delicious summer apples.

Apple Plant Diseases

Apple tree diseases can be a severe issue for gardeners and fruit farmers. These conditions can weaken the plant, reduce the yield of apples, and even lead to death in extreme cases. The most common include apple scab, fire blight, and powdery mildew.

Apple scab is caused by a fungus that causes leaf and fruit deformities. Fire blight is a bacterial infection that quickly browns, and wilts leaves, producing oozing cankers on infected twigs. Finally, powdery mildew coats leave a thin layer of white fuzz, making them prone to curl or distort the shape. It's important to understand how to prevent apple plant diseases since they are difficult to cure once they occur.

Preventative methods are the best way to protect against these illnesses. All plants should be regularly inspected for early signs of disease, such as dead buds and yellow or brown leaf spots.

Additionally, proper watering techniques and pruning diseased branches can help maintain healthy growth. For more advanced infections, fungicides may also be used if deemed necessary by a certified arborist or tree care specialist. Taking preventative measures is essential in preserving apple trees and avoiding more serious health issues in the future.

Apple trees need space to thrive, so it's important to not overcrowd them. Apple trees are especially susceptible to various pests and diseases, many of which can be transferred to apples through neighbouring plants.

When planting around apple trees, steer clear of members of the tomato family, such as tomatoes, potatoes, and eggplants. These plants are prone to the same fungal diseases that affect apples, so they can easily spread these diseases if planted too close together.

It would be best to avoid pansies, geraniums, and coleus because these plants tend to be hosts for apple scabs. If apple scab is present in nearby plants, it will likely spread to your apple trees and cause them harm. Keeping your apple tree healthy is essential to produce abundant fruit, so stick to planting vegetables, fruits, and flowers that won't pose a disease risk when near your tree.

That said, apples may be one of the most helpful companion fruits one can plant in a garden, as they make an excellent choice to provide extra nutrition and protection to an area.

Companion fruit plants that can be planted around apple trees have similar benefits regarding soil and pest protection. Grapes and raspberries, for example, can help keep away harmful pests while providing much-needed ground cover to improve soil conditions near apple trees.

Strawberries are another excellent option for adding supplemental nitrogen to the soil as well as providing fragrant blooms that attract beneficial pollinators like bees. With so many options available, companion fruit plants are not only a great way to protect your apple trees from adverse elements, but it's also a fantastic way to get more use out of your gardening space.

HOW TO SOW APPLES

Correct Season to Sow Apples

Growing apples is a rewarding experience, but the correct season plays an important role in its successful growth. As they are usually deciduous trees, the ideal time to sow their seeds is from late autumn until early spring.

The season should not be too cold or hot - the seeds won't grow correctly when it snows and frosts. Fertile and well-drained soil with full sunlight can yield the best results - a mixture of earthworms, organic compost, and mulch will help boost their growth. Apples grown at the right time of year have the most delicious flavors, making them a perfect snack to serve over the summer.

Plant Needs and Requirements

Planting apple trees from seeds is an adventure that can bring incredible rewards - delicious and healthy apples. To start, it is important to choose the right kind of seed. Look for a variety that grows well in the local climate, your soil type and is resistant to pests.

The next step is to prepare the seeds for planting. This can be done by stratifying the seeds, which involves keeping them cold and wet so they awaken from their dormancy, or by breaking the seed coat with sandpaper or nicking with a knife.

When planting the apple seeds, do so in individual pots or trays filled with quality soil. Make sure to place each seed about an inch beneath the soil's surface. Provide warmth and moisture for your seeds to thrive - keep your soil damp but not soggy so that it won't dry out too quickly or grow mold and fungus due to over-watering.

Apple seeds, like most plants, have specific temperature requirements for optimal germination. Apple seeds tend to germinate best at temperatures between 60°F and 75°F.

Temperatures outside of this range can make it more diffi-cult for the seed to sprout or cause the seedling to have weak or stunted growth. Nevertheless, keeping the optimal temperature within the mentioned range can increase the seedling's chances of flourishing into healthy apple trees.

When it comes to ensuring that a newly planted apple tree will thrive, the timing of the transplant is just as important as the soil and location. Apple seedlings should be moved from their original container when they reach a height of 6 inches and have three or four true leaves.

The transplant should take place in the late spring or early summer months when there is enough sunlight for photosynthesis and access to plenty of soil nutrients. This also allows the young tree plenty of time to settle into its new home and begin fairing actively before the onset of cooler weather.

Additionally, always check the root system before planting - healthy roots should appear white in color and firmly clumped together. Avoid any plants with wilting roots or discoloration.

To help ensure a successful transplantation, you'll want to choose a space with plenty of water drainage and prepare the soil before planting the seedling. With some basic knowledge of when and where to plant your apple seedling, you'll have a happy, healthy tree that will bear fruit in no time.

Spacing and Measurement

Transplanting apple seedlings is an activity that requires precision and accuracy to get a successful crop at the end of the season. Achieving optimal space between each tree is essential to ensure they have access to water and nutrients in the soil and adequate sunlight exposure.

It's also important to ensure its root system has enough room to grow and develop. Poor spacing of apple trees can lead to competition for resources, over-crowding, and ultimately prevent the fruit from ripening properly or reaching its full potential.

Additionally, as trees grow, physical contact with surrounding trees or walls can cause fractures in the bark, and in extreme cases, whole limbs may be broken off. Accurately measuring out the space per tree is a crucial step in successfully planting an apple orchard that will yield high-quality fruit for many years.

Planting apple seedlings may seem like an intimidating task, but with just a few simple steps, it doesn't have to be. To ensure your seedlings get ample space for growth and good light exposure, it is important to adhere to optimal spacing and measurements when planting.

Each seedling should be planted 12-15 feet between each seedling. When digging the hole for the seedlings, this should be about twice as wide as the tree's root ball and roughly as deep so that the main root stem remains at the soil level.

Compost or well-aged manure should also be mixed in with the existing soil in equal amounts when backfilling the hole to ensure it retains enough moisture while fostering healthy growth.

While it may take some patience and planning to get your apple trees in the ground correctly, once you've followed these steps, you're well on your way to growing a luscious bounty.

MAINTAINING YOUR APPLES

Maintaining your apple trees is vital to ensuring a fruitful harvest season. Regular pruning, watering, and careful inspections can help your trees stay healthy and disease-free.

If you are lucky enough to have an apple tree in the back-yard, you will definitely want it to provide bushels of juicy fruit every year, and unfortunately that won't happen if it isn't properly maintained.

But maintaining apple trees isn't just about having fresh apples - it also helps create a healthy ecosystem in your garden/backyard and share the bounty with your local wildlife, as birds and other animals may rely on the ripe fruits throughout the year.

With the many benefits of growing an apple tree, such as fresh seasonal fruit, magnificent blossoms in the spring, and shade and shelter during the winter, maintaining your apple trees is a must.

Pruning and Thinning Your Apple Trees

Pruning and thinning apple trees is an important part of their care. This ensures the tree's health and helps you get a better crop of fruit each year.

Pruning involves removing dead and diseased branches and shaping them for optimal fruit production. Thinning removes parts that develop too close together to improve circulation and potential light exposure for each apple.

With proper pruning and thinning, an apple tree can be healthier and live much longer than if these steps were not taken. In addition to its health benefits to the tree, it also makes for bigger and more succulent apples to enjoy throughout the year.

The best time to prune apple trees is during their dormant period in late winter or early spring before the buds have begun to swell. Thinning should occur after the petals have dropped off but before the fruits show color. When pruning, it's important to remove any dead or diseased branches, as well as branches taking energy away from healthy growth around the tree's center.

It's also important to open up your tree's canopy so that sunlight can reach near-ground branches and allow for better air circulation.

When thinning apple trees, be sure to leave no more than 4 apples per cluster so that each remaining fruit gets enough space and nutrients to grow properly - with both tasks, it's important to use sharp pruning tools.

Following these best practices should help set you up for success in producing a good crop of apples.

Watering Apples

Properly watering apple trees is crucial to producing a healthy harvest of fruit. Apple trees require moist soil for their roots to absorb nutrients and water efficiently. When the soil gets too dry, the tree will experience stress which can lead to dropping leaves and fruit, as well as weaker growth.

Watering too frequently or too much can drown the roots and deprive them of oxygen, causing a decline. The key is to water deeply but infrequently, allowing the soil to dry out slightly between waterings.

A good rule of thumb is to apply enough water to moisten the soil to a depth of 2 to 3 feet. This typically means watering until you see it pooling, then stopping and allowing it to soak in.

Water at the tree's base, avoiding spraying the leaves - this will encourage the roots to grow deeper, making the tree more drought-tolerant.

Fertilization For Apples

Apples are among the most popular fruits enjoyed around the world, with many different varieties to choose from. Most people don't realize that apple trees require proper fertilization to produce healthy and fresh fruit.

Adequate fertilization helps to ensure a healthy and bountiful apple harvest, as plants that lack sufficient nutrient intake struggle to reach their full potential. Fertilizers supplement the existing nutrient reserves within the soil, ensuring that the tree's roots can access key minerals and vitamins needed for stronger growth and greater yields of sweet, juicy fruits.

Furthermore, fertilizer has a major effect on the total amount of fruit produced by the tree, ensuring that we get more bang for our buck when harvesting apples. With proper fertilization techniques, we can enjoy an almost unlimited supply of delicious apples as well as an abundance of nutrition.

When it comes to fertilizing apple trees, the type of fertilizer you should use will depend on the tree's age and variety. Generally, you should use a balanced fertilizer such as 10-10-10 or 12-12-12. For young trees, they need more phosphorus than nitrogen, so a fertilizer with higher levels of phosphorus, like 5-10-5 or 6-14-4, is recommended.

For more established trees, fertilization is required once in the spring before buds break and then again three months later to help boost new growth and flower production.

Be sure to water regularly after application and ensure not to over-fertilize, which can result in salt build-up and damage to the root system.

For those who prefer to grow their bounty of apple trees without relying on synthetic chemicals, organic fertilizer can be a great way to help apple trees get the nutrients they need to thrive.

Organic fertilizers deliver nutrients to your trees slowly and steadily, which allows them to be absorbed more efficiently than synthetic fertilizers.

Look for a fertilizer specifically designed for fruit growing - these will typically contain calcium, magnesium, and zinc, all of which help promote healthier growth and development of the tree.

Additionally, you'll want an organic fertilizer with plenty of nitrogen, such as fish emulsion or kelp meal, to help stimulate root development and increases photosynthesis within the foliage.

Compost and manure is an excellent option for providing extra nutrients that natural soil may lack. Additionally, vermicompost, a compost made of worm casts, can be used with other soil amendments like wood ash or lime.

The best time to use an organic fertilizer is after planting in the spring and then again in late summer for optimum growth. During late summer, if your plants seem to be growing slowly or show signs of nutrient deficiency, such as yellowing leaves, you can also add organic fertilizer during this time. All these methods are designed to provide just the right balance of nutrition for your apple trees to reach their full potential.

PROTECTING YOUR APPLES

Extreme Temperatures

Protecting your apple fruit trees from extreme temperatures is essential for a successful harvest. Depending on your climate, tree protection might range from simple pruning practices to complex irrigation systems.

To start, consider enhancing the growth of your trees by adding mulch and nutrient-rich soil around their trunks to insulate them against extreme cold.

Windbreak barriers and frost cloths are also helpful for either hot or cold climates – they can deflect harsh sunlight during summer months or trap heat underneath a row of trees to help them better withstand freezing temperatures during winter.

If possible, install drip irrigation to ensure the trees receive regular water, especially during the hotter seasons. Additionally, insect infestations and diseases should be monitored closely during excessive heat or dry spells, as environmental conditions promote these occurrences.

Taking these steps will help keep your apple fruit trees protected during extreme temperatures and allow them to yield a bountiful harvest.

Protecting Apples From Pest

Protecting an apple tree from pests is often a priority for any apple grower. The damage caused by pests can dramatically reduce the tree yield, causing major economic losses for orchard owners.

Luckily, several methods can be used to protect these trees from infestations. Regular inspections should be made to identify any signs of pest activity early on, such as tunnels chewed in leaves or larvae on branches.

If a pest problem is identified, it's essential to act fast and use effective integrated pest management practices like employing natural predators and biological pesticides to eliminate the problem without harming other beneficial insects or birds.

In some cases, physical barriers like insect netting may also need to be deployed. Early detection is key in preventing severe damage caused by these insects.

Sanitation practices like deep pruning, removing old fruit and leaves, and controlling weeds in the area can help maintain your tree's general health. For example, ants and other insects like spider mites will often travel up dead branches and lay eggs where they can more easily spread throughout the tree.

Spraying with water usually eliminates the problem of spider mites which tend to attack apple trees when conditions are dry. Additionally, introducing beneficial insects may help keep a close watch against pest incursions.

Taking advantage of these simple yet effective measures can help protect your apple tree while preserving its beauty and bounty.

HARVESTING APPLES

Apple trees can take a few years before they start to produce fruit. It usually takes three to four years for an apple tree to mature and begin producing a crop of apples, but ultimately the harvest time varies depending on the type of tree and climate.

Some areas in cooler climates may require longer growing season times for apple trees, especially compared to regions with milder climates. Some dwarf trees have much shorter maturation times, taking only one year from sapling to harvest.

Pruning, fertilizing, and providing adequate water are key elements in creating optimal growing conditions to help ensure successful growth and an earlier harvest time.

Harvesting apples from fruit trees can be a rewarding experience, as well as a tasty treat. Firstly, apples should be picked when firm and red with no soft spots. Wisps of straw under the apple indicate it is ripe.

All fruits should be handled gently while picking to extend their shelf life. Before harvesting, prune the branches of any leaves or old fruit that may have been left behind. In addition to harvesting with hands, using a shaking pole can quickly break loose any fruit not readily picked by hand.

The most important part about harvesting is ensuring that you don't over-pick or damage the branch or trunk of the tree in any way - this will ensure your apple tree stays healthy for all future harvests.

Make sure to pick apples before any animals have had a chance to also take their share. With careful attention and preparation, harvesting apples from your own fruit tree can give you plenty of delicious snacks and share your bounty with friends and family.

SAVING APPLE SEEDS

Apple seeds are easy to harvest from the comfort of your home. All it takes is a little elbow grease and some basic tools like a knife, bowl, and spoon. First, start by selecting fresh, ripe apples for the clearest, strongest seeds. Use a sharp knife to cut the apple vertically, exposing the core with several divided chambers of small crunchy white apple seeds.

Scoop out each chamber and place the seeds into your bowl. Rinse off any excess chunks of fruit residue from the seeds, then let them air dry on paper towels or in a breathable mesh container.

Store them in an air-tight bag or container at room temperature to maximize their shelf life. Apple seeds should be sealed completely away from moisture and light, as these two elements are detrimental to their survival.

Additionally, they should not be stored in plastic wrapping or other materials that may contain chemicals - instead, use a clean paper towel or light cloth as a barrier between your container and the seeds. With proper storage techniques, your apple seeds should remain viable for many years.

CHAPTER 5

GROWING YOUR SUMMER STRAWBERRIES

T here's something special about biting into a juicy, ripe strawberry that was just plucked minutes ago from your very own garden. Not only do they taste better, but there are other benefits to growing your own summer strawberries.

For one, you have the peace of mind of knowing exactly what chemicals, if any, were used during the growing process. Plus, it's a fun activity that can involve the whole family, especially kids who love to help out in the garden.

These little red berries are also packed with nutrients that are good for your health - rich in vitamin C, fiber, and antioxidants, which are a delicious and healthy addition to any diet.

On top of that, let's not forget about the cost savings - buying fresh strawberries from the store can be expensive, but growing your own can save you money in the long run. With a bit of time and effort, growing your summer strawberries can be a rewarding experience that pays off with every sweet bite.

THE RIGHT SOIL FOR STRAWBERRIES

If you're planning on growing strawberries, the importance of testing your soil cannot be overstated. Without knowing the nutrient content, pH level, and other important soil factors, it's nearly impossible to determine what your strawberry plants need to thrive.

Even if your soil looks rich and healthy, it may lack key nutrients or have an imbalanced pH level. By taking the time to test your soil, you can make informed decisions about preparing it for the best possible strawberry harvest.

Whether you're a seasoned gardener or just starting out, investing in a soil test can make all the difference in the success of your strawberry crop.

Growing summer strawberries requires the accurate soil conditions to ensure a rich harvest. Sandy-loamy soil is ideal for strawberries as it provides great airflow and allows water to drain efficiently.

Adding compost, manure, or fertilizer to the soil can help provide essential nutrients for the plants to grow strong and healthy. It's also important to ensure the soil has a pH level between 5.5 and 6.5 for optimal growth.

This will help ensure that your strawberry plants absorb all the necessary nutrients for robust growth and a bountiful summer harvest.

While it may be tempting to use whatever soil is readily available, there are some types you should avoid. For starters, steer clear of any soil that is dense or heavy.

This can make it challenging for the roots to establish themselves and absorb the necessary nutrients. Additionally, avoid planting strawberries in consistently wet or compacted soil, as this can promote disease and hinder fruit development. With the right soil conditions, growing summer strawberries can be a fun and rewarding experience.

Strawberries Plant Diseases

Strawberries are a beloved fruit enjoyed worldwide, but unfortunately, they are susceptible to a range of plant diseases. These diseases can impact the health and yield of the plant and even result in the death of the entire crop. Some of the common types of strawberry plant diseases include gray mold, powdery mildew, and leaf spot.

Gray mold is caused by the fungus Botrytis cinerea and causes a soft, grayish mold to develop on the strawberries.

Powdery mildew, caused by the fungus Sphaerotheca macularis, appears as white powdery patches on the leaves and fruit of the plant.

Leaf spot is caused by the fungus Mycosphaerella fragariae and causes purple or brown spots on the leaves.

To prevent these diseases, it's essential to practice good sanitation and hygiene, choose healthy plants, and adequately manage the environment in which the strawberries are grown.

Maintaining good air circulation and avoiding wetting the leaves when watering is crucial. Additionally, removing any infected plant parts and using organic fungicides can help keep your strawberries healthy and thriving.

By being proactive in preventing strawberry plant diseases, you can ensure a bountiful harvest of sweet and juicy berries.

When growing strawberries, it's important to consider the plants that shouldn't be placed around them. Some common culprits include tomatoes, peppers, and eggplants, all of which belong to the same family as the potato plant.

These plants can introduce soil-borne diseases and pests that can wreak havoc on your strawberry plants, potentially stunting their growth or causing them to wither away.

Additionally, avoid planting brassica family members, such as broccoli, cauliflower, and Brussels sprouts, as they can produce toxic chemicals in strawberries.

However certain companion plants can improve the growth and flavor of strawberries. Not only do these plants look great together, but they can also benefit each other in a number of ways.

For example, planting blueberry bushes around your strawberry patch can help to deter birds from snacking on your juicy red fruit. Additionally, blueberry plants thrive in acidic soil, just like strawberries, making them natural companions in the garden.

Another great option is planting raspberries near your strawberries. These two fruits complement each other in taste and growing conditions, and together they make for a visually stunning berry patch.

Whatever companion plants you choose, make sure to do some research and select ones that will thrive in your growing conditions and complement your strawberry harvest.

HOW TO SOW STRAWBERRIES

Correct Season to Sow Strawberries

When it comes to cultivating sweet and juicy strawberries, timing is everything, and the season you decide to plant can mean the difference between a successful and disappointing harvest.

Fortunately, strawberry plants are adaptable and can thrive in a range of seasons, depending on the climate and region. The best time to plant strawberries is early spring, as soon as the soil can be worked so they have time to establish roots and foliage before the heat of summer arrives.

However, if you live in a cooler climate, late summer or early fall may be a better season to grow strawberries, as this allows for a longer growing season and larger fruit. Regardless of the season, strawberries require plenty of sunlight and well-draining soil to reach their full potential. With proper care and attention, you can enjoy a bountiful crop of these delicious berries for years to come.

Plant Needs and Requirements

Germinating strawberry seeds can be a fun and rewarding experience for any gardener. To start, it's essential to ensure you have good quality seeds and proper equipment. Strawberry seeds require plenty of light and moisture to germinate successfully.

First, choose the right seeds - look for varieties that are best suited to your specific climate and growing conditions. Once you have collected your seeds, soak them in water for several hours. This will help the seeds shed their protective coating and boost their chances of sprouting.

Next, plant your seeds about an inch deep in a high-quality seed-starting mix, ensuring they are evenly spaced and lightly covered with soil. Be sure to water consistently, keeping the soil moist but not too wet.

In order to give your seeds the best chance of germination, it's important to keep them in a controlled environment with proper moisture levels and temperature. While the ideal temperature for strawberry seed germination can vary by variety, most seeds require a range of 60-70 degrees Fahrenheit to sprout.

Strawberry seedlings are ready to be transplanted when they have at least 3-4 true leaves and are around 2-3 inches tall. This usually happens about a month after germination.

When it's time to transplant, make sure to choose a sunny, well-draining spot with rich soil. Also, don't forget to water your seedlings regularly and keep an eye out for pests or diseases that could harm your crop.

By following these tips, you'll be well on your way to harvesting sweet, juicy strawberries that you can enjoy all summer long.

Spacing and Measurement

When it comes to transplanting strawberry seedlings, spacing and measurements may seem like a mundane task. However, it is actually critical to their growth and success.

Proper spacing allows each plant to have enough room to grow and spread out its roots, accessing the necessary nutrients and water, as well as helping with pest control by allowing for adequate airflow between the plants.

Measuring the distance between each plant ensures an even distribution and avoids overcrowding, which can lead to poor fruit production and the spread of disease. Without these precise steps, seedlings can easily become stressed and stunted, hindering their ability to reach their full potential.

Taking the time to properly space and measure when transplanting strawberry seedlings is a small task that yields big rewards.

When planting strawberry seedlings, it's important to remember the desired spacing and measurements to ensure a fruitful harvest. Generally, each seedling should be spaced about 12-24 inches apart, with each row being separated by about 3-4 feet. This allows for plenty of room for the plants to grow and spread while also allowing easy access for pruning and harvesting.

It's also important to ensure the holes for the seedlings are deep enough, as the plant crown should sit just above the soil's surface. With the correct spacing and measurements, your strawberry patch will thrive and produce delicious berries for years to come.

MAINTAINING YOUR STRAWBERRIES

Maintaining your strawberry plant is crucial if you want to reap its sweet rewards. Not only does taking care of your plant improve its overall health, but it also ensures a bountiful harvest.

Consistently checking for pests or diseases, watering and fertilizing regularly, and pruning accordingly are all crucial tasks that contribute to the success of your strawberry plant. Neglecting these tasks could result in a weaker plant and smaller, less flavorful fruits.

By giving your plants the attention it deserves, you'll be rewarded with not just a tasty fruit but also a flourishing garden full of life. So take pride in your green thumb, and don't forget to nurture those strawberry plants.

Pruning and Thinning Your Strawberries

Strawberries are a much-loved fruit for their sweetness and versatility in culinary dishes. To ensure they grow successfully, pruning and thinning your strawberry plants is crucial.

When left unattended, strawberry plants can become overcrowded and prone to disease, ultimately leading to smaller fruit yields. Thinning your plants allows for better airflow and light penetration, leading to more vigorous, healthier plants.

Additionally, trimming back foliage and dead leaves improves plant health, makes for easier harvesting come the fruiting season, and allows more space for new growth.

As a strawberry grower, you may wonder when and how to prune and thin your plants. Knowing when to can help your plants produce better fruits and maintain their health.

The ideal time to prune your strawberries is in early spring, after the last frost date in your area. This ensures you are not cutting back any new growth or flower buds. To prune your plants, remove any dead, diseased, or damaged branches using sharp and clean shears.

Make sure to cut them close to the base of the plant. Thinning, on the other hand, should be done in the summer once the strawberries are ripening.

Thinning involves removing any weak or crowded stems to allow better airflow and light penetration. This should be done when the strawberry plants have about five or six leaves. By following these simple steps, you can ensure your strawberry plants will produce juicy, delicious fruits season after season.

Watering Strawberries

Proper hydration is crucial for any plant's growth, but it is especially essential for succulent and delicate strawberry plants. Moisture helps uptake nutrients, photosynthesis, and blooming of the fruit.

Adequate watering ensures that your garden strawberry plants have a sufficient water supply, creating the perfect conditions for growth and yield.

Overwatering or underwatering can adversely affect the strawberries, causing root rot, mildew, and other diseases. Be mindful of the soil moisture level and establish the correct watering routine for your plants.

Proper watering techniques, such as watering deeply and slowly, can help your strawberry plants grow strong and healthy. Healthy, nourished strawberries are worth the effort, and correctly watering your plants ensures a generous harvest of beautiful and delicious fruits.

The key to watering your strawberry plants is to strike a balance between not underwatering and overwatering. Strawberries need to be consistently moist but not water-logged to grow healthy and sweet.

To ensure adequate hydration, give your strawberry plants an inch of water per week, either by hand- or drip irrigation at the base of the plant. Avoid spraying the leaves or flowers with water, as this can lead to rot or fungal growth.

Finally, check the soil frequently to make sure it remains consistently moist but not soggy. By following these simple tips, you can provide your strawberry plants with the right amount of hydration they need to produce a bountiful crop.

Fertilization For Strawberries

As any gardener knows, providing the right nutrients to your plants is essential for healthy growth and abundant harvests. When it comes to growing delicious and juicy strawberries, fertilization is key.

Without the proper nutrients, these beloved fruits can be small and flavorless. Fertilizers provide essential elements like nitrogen, phosphorus, and potassium that help promote healthy growth and development.

With the right amount of fertilizer, strawberry plants can produce more abundant fruits, ensuring a bountiful harvest for strawberry lovers everywhere. Not only does fertilization improve the quality of the fruit, but it can also increase the overall yield of the plant.

Additionally, fertilization aids the fruit in developing essential vitamins and minerals that make them tasty and nutritious.

When it comes to strawberry plants, choosing the right type of fertilizer and knowing when to use it is particularly important.

Nitrogen, phosphorus, and potassium are the three essential nutrients that strawberries need for strong roots, healthy foliage, and juicy fruit. However, the timing of their application can make all the difference.

To ensure optimal growth and yield, applying a balanced fertilizer such as NPK 12-12-12 when planting your strawberries and again in the fall after the last fruit has been harvested is best. Avoid using high-nitrogen fertilizers after the flowering stage, as this can lead to excessive vegetative growth at the expense of fruit production.

Many gardeners see the benefits of using fertilizers to give their plants a boost. However, it's important to understand the types of fertilizers available. There are two main types of fertilizers available on the market - organic and synthetic.

Organic fertilizers, such as compost or manure, are made from natural materials and are known for being slow-release, providing plants with a range of nutrients over an extended period.

On the other hand, synthetic fertilizers are produced chemically and offer rapid nutrient delivery to plants. While both have their pros and cons, it's important to note that some gardeners prefer organic fertilizers since they're considered more environmentally friendly.

Still, it ultimately depends on the individual's preferences and circumstances. Regardless of your choice, your strawberry plants will be healthy, productive, and delicious with the right fertilizing practices.

PROTECTING YOUR STRAWBERRIES

Extreme Temperatures

If you're a strawberry lover, you know that there's nothing better than sweet, juicy berries plucked fresh from your very own garden. But when temperatures soar or plunge, your precious plants can suffer, and your harvest may be jeopardized.

Luckily, there are some simple strategies you can use to protect your strawberry plants from extreme temperatures. For hot weather, provide plenty of shade and make sure the soil stays moist.

During cold snaps, cover your plants with a frost blanket or even a blanket or sheet to keep them warm. With a bit of care and attention, your strawberry plants will thrive and reward you with a delicious bounty of fruit.

Using mulch is a great way to help regulate soil temperature, as it helps to retain moisture, suppress weed growth, and prevent erosion.

By adding a layer of mulch around your strawberry plants, you'll be providing them with the protection they need to survive those scorching hot days or freezing cold nights.

Plus, as an added bonus, mulch can add nutrients to your soil as it breaks down over time. By taking the necessary precautions, you can ensure that your strawberry plants remain healthy and thrive in any weather conditions.

Protecting Strawberries From Pest

Strawberries are a delicious and healthy addition to any garden, but unfortunately, they are also highly susceptible to pest attacks. The most common pests that invade strawberry plants are aphids, spider mites, slugs, and snails.

These pests can cause significant damage to the plant, including stunted growth, deformed leaves, and even death. However, with proper preventative measures, you can keep your strawberry plants thriving and pest-free.

One effective way to prevent pest attacks is by regularly inspecting the plants for any signs of infestation and promptly removing any affected areas.

Additionally, you can apply organic insecticides, such as neem oil or garlic spray, to deter pests from attacking your strawberry plants. Planting insect-repelling plants like marigolds, which emit a scent that deters many pests, is a known and effective way to deter common pests.

Adhering to good gardening practices and hygiene, for example, removing dead plant matter, weeding regularly, planting in well-drained soil, providing proper nutrition, and watering consistently, can ultimately eliminate the chances of pest attacks occurring initially.

HARVESTING STRAWBERRIES

If you're eager to enjoy the delicious taste of freshly harvested strawberries, you might be wondering how long it takes for strawberry plants to mature. The good news is that strawberry plants are relatively fast-growing, and most varieties can start producing fruit in just a few months.

Generally, you can expect to start seeing strawberries on your plants about 4-6 weeks after the first flowers emerge. However, the size and quality of your berries will improve as the plants mature, so it's often worth waiting a bit longer for a bigger, juicier harvest.

Most strawberry plants take around three to four months to produce it's signature deep red fruit after planting. So with a little patience and care, you'll be munching on fresh, homegrown strawberries in no time.

Harvesting sweet and juicy strawberries straight from your garden can be a fulfilling experience for any fruit grower. But before you start plucking those red berries, knowing the right method for picking them is important.

To harvest strawberry fruit plants, begin by identifying the ripe fruits that are fully red and plump. Gently cup the berry in your hand and carefully twist and pull it from the plant using your fingers.

Try not to tug too hard or damage the stem, as this can lead to the plant producing fewer fruits. If the stem does not release the fruit easily, use gardening shears to cut the stem just above the fruit.

The best time to harvest strawberries is in the morning when temperatures are cooler, and the fruits are firm. Remember to only pick the ripe ones and leave the unripe berries on the plant to avoid stunting growth. By following these simple tips, you can enjoy a bountiful harvest of delicious strawberries all season long.

SAVING STRAWBERRY SEEDS

If you're a lover of strawberries and want to try your hand at growing them yourself, you might consider harvesting your own strawberry seeds. However, the process isn't as easy as simply plucking the seeds out of the fruit.

First, gather some ripe strawberries and mash them up in a bowl. Add water to the bowl, and stir it gently. Let the mixture sit for about three days, stirring occasionally. Once the mixture has developed a layer of mold on top, it's time to strain out the seeds. Rinse them off and pat them dry.

If you've ever wanted to grow your delicious strawberries from scratch, knowing how to properly store the seeds is certainly important. After all, the success of your future plants largely depends on the quality of the seeds you use.

To start, good storage conditions are essential. Keep them in a cool, dry place away from sunlight, moisture, or extreme temperatures. You may also want to store them in an airtight container, such as a jar or plastic bag.

Another tip is to label the container with the date and variety of the seeds to avoid confusion. By following these simple steps, you'll be on your way to growing your very own strawberry plants in no time.

CHAPTER 6
GROWING YOUR SUMMER KIWIFRUIT

G rowing your own summers, Kiwis can offer many benefits beyond just the sweet and tangy taste of the fruit itself. For starters, consuming fresh, home-grown produce is always a much healthier alternative to store-bought options that may have been treated with chemicals or preservatives.

Let's not forget the rewarding experience that allows you to connect with nature, making a positive environmental impact by reducing the carbon emissions associated with commercial farming and transportation - not to mention how kiwis are packed with essential vitamins and nutrients, as well as containing natural enzymes that aid in digestion and help with skin health. The benefits of growing your own Kiwi's fruits seem endless.

Kiwi plants are relatively easy to grow and require minimal maintenance. So, with the following steps and guidance, why not give it a try and enjoy your very own sweet and succulent summer Kiwis straight from your garden.

THE RIGHT SOIL FOR KIWIFRUIT

When it comes to cultivating any plant, it's important to set a strong foundation for success. This starts with examining the soil you plan to plant in - and the same goes for growing kiwis.

So why is testing your soil so crucial for these sweet fruits? Well, kiwis require a specific balance of nutrients and pH levels in order to grow and produce fruit healthily. Without testing your soil, you may not know what amendments you must make to ensure your kiwi plants thrive.

It can be tempting to skip this step, but testing your soil can save you disappointment and wasted effort. With the right foundation, your kiwi plants will be well on their way to producing delicious, juicy fruit.

Growing Kiwis can be a rewarding and delicious experience, but it all starts with suitable soil. Summer Kiwis require well-drained soil rich in nutrients like nitrogen, phosphorus, and potassium.

Using organic materials like compost, manure, or worm castings when planting Kiwis can help create the perfect environment needed for their growth. Additionally, having a soil pH between 5.0 and 6.5 is ideal. The soil needs to have proper water drainage to ensure that the roots do not become waterlogged, which can cause them to rot.

That said, it's just as important to understand the type of soil conditions that should also be avoided when growing Kiwis.

One of the soil types that should be avoided is heavy clay soil. This soil type is known to retain water and become compact, which can cause root rot and hinder the kiwi plant's growth.

Another type of soil to avoid is sandy soil. This type of soil drains water quickly, which can cause the Kiwi's roots to dry and damage.

As previously mentioned, organic matter-rich soils are ideal for kiwi plants as they provide the necessary nutrients and aeration. By selecting the right soil for your kiwi plants, you'll be sure to enjoy a bountiful harvest of juicy, delicious fruit.

Kiwifruit Plant Diseases

Kiwi plants are hardy and resilient, but just like any other living thing, they are susceptible to diseases. There are several types of kiwi plant diseases that you should be aware of, including canker, leaf spot, and bacterial blight.

Canker can cause stem and trunk damage, while leaf spot appears as small brown or red spots on the leaves. On the other hand, bacterial blight leads to the wilting and discoloration of leaves and can be fatal to the plant.

However, prevention is key when it comes to protecting your kiwi plants from diseases. Maintaining proper spacing between plants, pruning regularly, and avoiding overwatering can all help to prevent the spread of disease. Additionally, using disease-resistant kiwi varieties can also help to protect your plants from the onset of disease.

As gardeners, it is important to be mindful of which plants you're planting together. After all, some plants can thrive in each other's company, while others can actually become toxic to each other.

One plant you don't want to plant around kiwis is anything in the nightshade family, including tomatoes, peppers, and eggplants. That's because these plants naturally release solanine, a toxic compound that can severely damage the Kiwi's health.

Other plants to avoid include those with high nitrogen content, as they can lead to aggressive growth that will rob the Kiwi of necessary nutrients.

As previously mentioned, some plants do in fact thrive and are beneficial to your kiwi plants' yield and growth when grown in close proximity. Fortunately, there are a variety of fruits that can grow in harmony with kiwis, including strawberries, raspberries, blueberries, and blackberries.

These companion plants can help to improve soil quality, provide shade for the kiwi plants, and deter pests from attacking the kiwi vines. Additionally, having a variety of fruit plants in your garden will allow you to enjoy a bountiful harvest throughout the growing season.

Not only will it make your garden more visually appealing, but it will also provide you with delicious and nutritious fruits to enjoy.

HOW TO SOW KIWIFRUIT

Correct Season to Sow Kiwifruit

When cultivating your own Kiwi, it's important to know when the best time and season when to start planting.

Kiwi fruits are sensitive to frost, so they need to be planted during the early spring months, typically between March and May.

Planting too early can result in damage from late frosts, and planting too late can affect the growth and development of the fruit. Ensuring your planting season is correct is crucial to maximize your chances of a bountiful harvest.

Plant Needs and Requirements

Before you can enjoy the delicious and highly nutritious Kiwi fruits, you need to start with germinating Kiwi seeds into seedlings. It's important to also remember that growing Kiwi from seeds is a process that requires patience and attention.

Make to choose a seed variant specific to your growing climate, pest resistance, and the variety of Kiwi fruit you aim to grow. Be sure to use fresh kiwi seeds that have been cleaned and dried.

The first step is to soak the seeds in water for 24 hours, which will help break down the hard outer shell. Afterward, you'll need to prepare the planting medium, consisting of moist, well-draining soil.

Plant the seeds in a pot filled with rich soil, and place it in a sunny spot with good drainage. Make sure to keep the soil consistently moist but not too wet.

When it comes to temperature, kiwi seeds generally require a warm environment for germination. Ideally, temperatures within the range of 68°F to 77°F are suitable for kiwi seeds to sprout.

Anything below or above this range can negatively impact germination rates. So, if you're planning on growing kiwi from seeds, make sure to keep a close eye on the temperature to ensure the best possible start for your little seedlings.

While it's exciting to watch the little plantings sprout from their seeds, it's important to remember that they need time to build up their strength before being transplanted.

So, when exactly are they ready to be moved to a bigger pot or a garden plot? Typically, kiwi seedlings are ready to be transplanted when they have a few sets of true leaves and are about 3-4 inches tall. It's important to be gentle when handling the seedlings and to ensure their new environment has plenty of sunlight and well-draining soil. With a bit of careful observation and some TLC, you'll be well on your way to growing healthy, vigorous Kiwis that produce delicious fruit.

Spacing and Measurement

When it comes to transplanting kiwi seedlings, spacing, and measurements may not initially seem like a big deal. However, these details can make a significant impact on the success of your plants.

Proper spacing between seedlings allows each plant to grow and develop without competing for resources. Leaving insufficient room between plants may cause them to grow into each other, trapping moisture and increasing the risk of diseases such as powdery mildew.

Measurements ensure that the depth and width of each hole are suitable for the roots to establish themselves, leading to healthier and heartier plants. To avoid these pitfalls and set your kiwi seedlings up for success, make sure to pay close attention to spacing and measurements. The extra effort will pay off in the long run.

It is recommended to plant kiwi seedlings approximately 10 to 12 feet apart in rows that are spaced at least 14 feet apart. Make sure to dig a hole twice the size of the root system and deep enough to cover the entire root ball.

After planting, water the seedling thoroughly and cover the soil with a layer of organic mulch to help retain moisture. By following these guidelines, you can give your kiwi seedlings the best opportunity to thrive and provide you with a bountiful harvest.

MAINTAINING YOUR KIWIFRUIT

Maintaining your Kiwi trees is crucial if you want to enjoy sweet and succulent fruit. Kiwis are a popular fruit known for their juicy flesh and vibrant green texture. But unfortunately, these trees require a little extra TLC to ensure they grow properly.

If you don't care for your Kiwi trees, you could be looking at a potential loss of fruit or even worse, a dead tree. That's why it's important to put in the effort to maintain your Kiwi trees.

Regularly pruning your kiwi trees and taking care of the soil to ensure that they receive the right amount of water and nutrients is essential to promote growth and enhance the quality of the fruits.

By maintaining your kiwi trees, you can create a healthy and thriving garden and enjoy delicious fruits. So, roll up your sleeves, grab your tools, and get to work - your taste buds will thank you.

Pruning and Thinning Your Kiwifruit

Pruning and thinning your kiwi trees may seem like a tedious task, but it is incredibly important for the health and productivity of your plants.

By removing excess branches and fruits, you allow the tree to focus its energy on producing larger, juicier kiwis as it can receive more nutrients and sunlight. Not only will this result in a better harvest, but it will also prevent the tree from becoming overcrowded and diseased.

However, it's important to employ proper pruning techniques to avoid damaging the tree. Additionally, pruning helps maintain the shape and size of your kiwi trees, making it easier to harvest fruit due to less overcrowding.

So if you're looking to ensure a bountiful harvest and healthy kiwi trees, don't skip out on the practice of regular pruning and thinning.

The first step to successful kiwi tree pruning is to evaluate when to prune. It's best to prune in late winter or early spring while the tree is still dormant before new growth begins. This will ensure the tree has plenty of time to heal before the growing season begins.

As for how to prune, start by cutting back any dead or diseased branches, then thinning out any crossing branches that may rub against each other and cause damage. The goal is to create a well-structured and open canopy that allows plenty of sunlight to reach the fruit.

Not only will pruning and thinning your kiwi trees improve the tree's overall appearance, but it can also lead to a healthier harvest come the fruiting season, so don't be afraid to give it a trim.

Watering Kiwifruit

When it comes to growing kiwi trees, understanding the importance of proper watering techniques is crucial. Kiwi trees need consistent moisture levels to thrive, but over or under-watering can do more harm than good.

Too much water can lead to root rot and disease, while too little can result in stunted growth and unproductive trees. It's crucial to find the right balance, ensuring that the soil is moist but not soggy.

When it comes to watering your kiwi trees, timing is critical. It is important to water them deeply, allowing the water to penetrate the soil, reach the roots, and avoid getting water on the leaves or fruit, as this can lead to disease. Consistent watering is key, especially during hot, dry weather.

Kiwi trees prefer soil that is consistently moist but not waterlogged. To achieve this, water your kiwi trees once or twice a week, depending on rainfall and soil type, and make sure the water is soaking through to the tree's roots.

Give your kiwi trees enough water to moisten the soil to a depth of at least 6 inches. By taking the time to understand how much water your kiwi trees need and implementing a proper watering schedule, you can enjoy healthy, fruitful trees for years to come.

Fertilization For Kiwifruit

Kiwifruit is a popular fruit that is enjoyed by many people around the world. The key to obtaining its sweet, juicy flesh lies in the proper fertilization of kiwi fruit trees. Fertilization is the process of adding nutrients to the soil that help support the growth of the plant.

A well-fertilized kiwi fruit tree produces fruits that are not only tastier but also more abundant. That's why giving kiwi fruit trees the right amount and types of fertilizers they need to thrive is crucial. Without proper fertilization, the tree may suffer from stunted growth, weak branches, and a lower yield of fruits.

By ensuring that kiwi fruit trees are properly fertilized, gardeners can ensure that they can produce healthy, thriving, and abundance of succulent kiwi fruits.

The secret to a fruitful kiwi harvest lies in choosing the right fertilizer and applying it at the right time. Kiwi trees love nitrogen-rich fertilizers, but too much of it can result in excessive foliage growth at the expense of fruit production. To strike a balance, consider using a slow-release fertilizer that gradually releases nutrients over a period of time.

Organic fertilizers are a great type of slow-release fertilizer ideal for your Kiwi trees. Several types of organic fertilizers can benefit kiwi trees, including compost, manure, bone meal, and seaweed meal.

Compost provides a balanced mix of nutrients, while manure adds nitrogen to the soil.

Bone meal is high in phosphorus, which is crucial for fruit development, and seaweed meal offers a boost of trace minerals.

Organic fertilizers have the benefit of improving soil structure and microbial activity while also being environmentally friendly. In contrast, synthetic fertilizers have the advantage of being potent and providing plants with an instant boost of nutrients.

Ultimately, choosing between organic and synthetic fertilizers for Kiwi plants depends on personal preferences and the desired results.

As to when to apply fertilizer, it is recommended to do so in early spring, just as the buds start to emerge. This will give the tree a much-needed boost before the growing season begins. And don't forget to water regularly, especially during periods of drought, to help the tree absorb the nutrients and produce juicy, tasty kiwis.

PROTECTING YOUR KIWIFRUIT

Extreme Temperatures

Kiwis are a beloved fruit for many, known for their sweet, tangy flavor and bright green color. However, despite their popularity, kiwis are relatively delicate and can be easily damaged by extreme temperatures. High temperatures can damage the fruit, causing it to ripen too quickly or even rot, while low temperatures can cause frost damage.

To protect your kiwifruit from extreme temperatures, it is essential to have a well-established irrigation and drainage system in place, as well as proper crop management practices.

This includes pruning the vines to optimize airflow and ensuring the soil is sufficiently moist, which can help regulate the plant's temperature.

During colder months, consider wrapping the trunk and stems with protective material, such as burlap or blankets, to shield them from frost.

On hot, sunny days, it's essential to provide ample shade to prevent sun damage. This can be done by using shade cloth, erecting temporary structures, or planting trees that can act as natural shading.

Additionally, one of the best methods when it comes to protecting your kiwifruit from extreme temperatures is by utilizing mulch. Mulch not only insulates the plant's roots but also helps retain moisture, which is crucial for kiwi plants.

The ideal time to apply mulch is during the fall season when kiwis enter dormancy. Applying a layer of about 3-4 inches of organic mulch around the base of the plant can keep it warm in the winter and cool in the summer, preventing it from getting stressed out.

Moreover, mulch also suppresses weed growth, saves water, and adds nutrients to the soil as it breaks down. By taking these precautions, you can enjoy your kiwifruit all year round without worrying about weather-related damage.

Protecting Kiwifruit From Pest

Growing your own kiwi fruit tree is a rewarding experience, but it can also be challenging to protect it from pests.
These pesky critters are a familiar problem for most
gardeners, but with a little knowledge and some persistence, you can manage and prevent these pests from
invading your kiwi fruit tree.

Some of the most common pests to watch out for include
aphids, mites, scale insects, caterpillars, kiwi vine moths,
and the kiwi fruit fly. These pest feed on the leaves and
stems, causing extensive damage and weakening the plant,
as well as attacking the fruit, causing it to rot prematurely.

Fortunately, there are several steps you can take to prevent
these pests from destroying your kiwifruits. Firstly, it's
important to remember that prevention is key.

Regularly inspecting your tree for signs of damage and
pests is essential, where prompt action is required if
anything is detected. It's necessary to also maintain good
plant hygiene, where you can also introduce preventative
measures such as using an insecticidal spray, neem oil, or
applying a protective barrier around the roots.

Additionally, placing sticky traps around the base of the
tree to capture any unsuspecting insects is a great action
method, likewise employing organic control methods such
as companion planting and introducing beneficial insects
to your garden. You can protect your kiwi plants and enjoy
a generous harvest by taking the necessary precautions to
safeguard your Kiwi fruit tree.

HARVESTING KIWIFRUIT

Kiwi fruit trees are a unique and tasty addition to any garden, but many first-time growers are curious about how long it takes to bear fruit. While kiwi trees typically take longer to mature than other fruit trees, the wait is well worth it.

On average, kiwi fruit trees take about three to four years before they start producing fruit. However, this largely depends on the cultivar, growing conditions, and the tree's care.

With the right environment and care, the fruit-bearing age can be reduced to two and a half years. So if you plan on growing kiwi fruit trees, patience is key. The reward of harvesting sweet and juicy kiwis will be well worth the wait.

When it comes to harvesting kiwi fruit trees, timing is everything. The fruit should be picked only when it is fully ripe, which is signaled by a yield sign of sorts – the fruit should have a slightly soft feel to it and will detach easily from the vine.

Gentle handling is also vital - the kiwis should be carefully picked and carried in a soft container or basket to prevent bruising. You can also cut the stem with pruning shears leaving about an inch of stem attached to the fruit. You can always perform a taste test if you're unsure if it's time to harvest. Kiwis should be sweet and tangy and have a soft texture when ripe.

SAVING KIWIFRUIT SEEDS

Kiwifruit is a delicious fruit that is known for its juicy and sweet taste. If you are a kiwifruit lover, you might be wondering how to harvest the seeds so that you can grow your own plants.

Fortunately, this process is relatively simple and can be done with just a few household items. Start by cutting open a ripe kiwifruit and scooping the flesh into a bowl.

Rinse the seeds thoroughly to remove any excess fruit, then spread them out on a paper towel to dry.

Kiwi seeds are a precious commodity, and storing them properly is important to ensure their longevity. Once dry, place the seeds in an airtight container or a plastic bag and store them in a cool, dry location away from direct sunlight.

If stored correctly, kiwi seeds can remain viable for up to five years. These tiny seeds have the potential to grow into delicious kiwi plants, so treat them with care and watch your garden flourish.

CHAPTER 7

GROWING YOUR SUMMER WATERMELON

S ummertime is the season for juicy watermelons, and there's nothing quite like the satisfaction of enjoying a slice of fruit that you've grown in your very own garden. Not only does growing your own summertime watermelon give you a sense of pride and accomplishment, but it also offers a variety of health benefits. For one, you can be sure that your watermelon is free from harmful chemicals and pesticides.

Plus, it's a great source of hydration, vitamins, antioxidants, and fiber. You can choose to use organic methods or experiment with different varieties and growing techniques, tailoring your watermelon to your specific taste preferences. Nothing beats the taste of a sun-ripened watermelon that you've nurtured and cared for yourself.

So why not give it a try this summer and see just how sweet and delicious your homegrown watermelon can be. With a little bit of effort and patience, growing your own watermelon is a rewarding experience that yields delicious and nutritious fruit that you can enjoy all summer long.

THE RIGHT SOIL FOR WATERMELONS

Watermelons are a favorite summertime fruit loved by many. When cultivating these juicy delights, it is crucial to know what type of soil you are working with to achieve the highest yield possible.

By testing your soil before planting watermelons, you can determine the soil's pH levels, nutrient content, and water-holding capacity. These factors can make all the difference in the growth and taste of your watermelons.

Testing your soil also helps you avoid soil deficiencies or overabundance of certain nutrients that may affect the development of your plants. With the information gathered from soil testing, you can provide the ideal environment for your watermelon seeds or seedlings to grow and flourish.

When it comes to growing summer watermelons, choosing the right soil cannot be overstated. To achieve the optimal environment for watermelon growth, you should aim for well-draining soil that is rich in organic matter.

Sandy loam or loamy soils are ideal, as they allow for adequate drainage while also retaining enough moisture for the plant to grow.

Additionally, it's important to ensure the soil has a pH level of 6.0 to 6.8, as too much acidity can inhibit growth. By starting with nutrient-rich, well-draining soil, you can set the stage for a bountiful harvest of delicious, refreshing watermelons.

Growing watermelons requires the right kind of soil, as not all types are suitable for these juicy fruits. Gardeners should avoid soils with a high clay content, or that are too heavy, as this can lead to poor drainage and root rot.

Similarly, excessively sandy soils may not retain enough nutrients and moisture essential for the watermelon plant's growth. Avoiding acidic soils will prevent stunted growth and lower yield. With the right soil, your watermelons are sure to thrive and provide sweet, juicy satisfaction all summer long.

Watermelon Plant Diseases

Many people adore the tasty and refreshing fruit watermelon. However, like any other plant, watermelon plants are susceptible to various diseases that can ruin the crop.

The most common watermelon plant diseases include the fungal disease known as powdery mildew, Fusarium wilt, and Anthracnose. Powdery mildew is a fungal disease that can affect both leaves and fruits, while Fusarium wilt is a soil-borne disease that causes the plant to wilt and eventually die. Anthracnose is another fungal disease that causes dark spots on leaves and fruits.

These diseases can cause damage to the plant and reduce the yield of the fruit. To prevent these diseases, it is essential to practice good plant hygiene. This includes avoiding overcrowding of plants, rotating crops, and removing infected plants as soon as they are spotted. Additionally, using disease-resistant varieties of watermelon can also help prevent the spread of diseases.

When planning your garden, it's important to consider which plants should not be grown near each other. When it comes to watermelons, there are certain plants that should be avoided.

One of these plants is cucumber, as they are both members of the same family and could potentially cross-pollinate, leading to bitter-tasting watermelons.

Another plant to avoid growing near watermelons is any type of squash, such as zucchini or pumpkin. This is because they both attract the same type of pests, such as squash bugs and vine borers, which can damage both plants.

By being intentional about the plants you choose to grow alongside your watermelons, you can ensure they have the necessary resources to thrive.

Planting companion fruit plants around it can add a whole new level of flavor to your garden. One great option is to plant cantaloupe, which is a close relative of watermelon and has a similar growing season.

Not only will it complement the watermelon's sweet taste, but it can also help deter pests from attacking your plants. Another option is to plant strawberries, which have shallow roots and grow well in containers. Placing them alongside your watermelon can add a pop of color and provide a juicy, tart contrast to its sweetness.

Also, strawberries are known for their ability to attract pollinators, which can benefit all plants in your garden. Whatever companion fruit you choose, planting them alongside watermelon can create a harmonious and fruitful growing environment.

However, it's always a good idea to research which plants are compatible with each other before planting to ensure a successful harvest.

HOW TO SOW WATERMELONS

Correct Season to Sow Watermelons

Growing watermelons requires careful planning and consideration. It's important to choose the right season to grow this juicy fruit, and if you're not sure when that is, don't worry, we've got you covered.

Watermelons thrive in warm weather, so it's best to plant them when the soil temperature is above 70 degrees Fahrenheit. Typically, this means waiting until the winter frost has passed and planting in early to mid-summer.

Doing so will ensure your watermelons have plenty of time to mature and ripen before the cooler fall weather sets in. With the right seasonal timing and conditions, your watermelon plants will produce juicy, sweet fruit that is perfect for a hot summer day.

Plant Needs and Requirements

Watermelons are a staple of summertime snacks, and what better way to fully appreciate all they have to offer than by growing your own. Germinating watermelon seeds into seedlings can seem daunting at first, but with the right knowledge and a bit of patience, anyone can do it.

The first step is to soak the seeds overnight in warm water to soften their tough shells. Plant the seeds about an inch deep and moisten the soil while germinating.

Once the seedlings start to grow, thin them out and give each plant plenty of space to spread out. Watermelon plants require lots of water and nutrients, so be sure to fertilize regularly and water deeply.

Watermelon seeds typically germinate at temperatures between 70-85°F. While this may seem like a broad range, it's important to note that soil temperature is just as important as air temperature in this process.

So, whether you're planting them in a garden or a pot, make sure to keep the soil temperature at a consistent level within this range to ensure successful germination and growth.

Watermelon seedlings are a joy to watch as they emerge from the soil and reach toward the sky. But when exactly are they ready to be moved from their nursery pots and transplanted into the garden?

Once your watermelon seedlings have sprouted and developed their first true leaves, it's time to start thinking about transplantation. Generally, this occurs when the seedlings are around 2-3 inches tall, which typically coincides with about 2-3 weeks after germination.

However, paying close attention to your particular seedlings and the conditions they're growing in is important. If they look a bit taller or have developed more leaves than this timeline, you can certainly transplant them earlier. With patience and care, you can ensure that your watermelon seedlings thrive and produce a abundant harvest.

Spacing and Measurement

Whether you're an experienced or novice gardener, it's crucial to understand the importance of spacing and measurements when transplanting watermelon seedlings. Proper spacing means allowing enough room for each plant to grow and spread out without competing for resources.

Plus, measuring the distance between each seedling ensures they are evenly spaced for optimal growth and a healthy harvest. Neglecting to plan out spacing and measurements can result in overcrowded plants, stunted growth, and, ultimately lower productivity. So, take the time to carefully calculate and measure the spacing between your watermelon seedlings - you'll be rewarded with juicy, plump fruits come harvest time.

When it comes to planting watermelon seedlings, spacing and measurements are crucial aspects to consider. To ensure optimal growth and yield, it's recommended to space seedlings at least 3 feet apart in rows that are up to 8 feet apart.

This will give each plant enough room to spread out and receive adequate sunlight and nutrients. Additionally, the soil should be tilled to a depth of at least 6 inches to allow the roots to establish themselves properly.

It's also important to plant the seedlings in well-draining soil with plenty of organic matter and to keep the soil consistently moist throughout the growing season.

Paying attention to spacing and measurements in the early stages of growing watermelon will set you up for success as the plants mature and produce juicy, delicious fruit.

MAINTAINING YOUR WATERMELONS

Cultivating watermelon plants can be a gardener's dream come true. Not only do they produce delicious and refreshing fruit, but they also add a pop of vibrant green to any garden. However as much as we'd like for these refreshing fruits to grow with independence and harvest when ready – this simply isn't the case.

Maintenance of your watermelon plant is key and there are many reasons why it is important to maintain your watermelon plants - the most obvious one being the quality of the fruit. A well-maintained watermelon plant will produce juicy and delicious fruit that is bursting with flavor.

Neglecting your plants, however, can lead to stunted growth, poor fruit quality, and even plant disease. The maintenance process includes regular watering, proper fertilization, thinning, and pruning to promote healthy growth. With proper maintenance, you can ensure the success of your watermelon harvest and enjoy the sweet taste of success.

Pruning and Thinning Your Watermelons

Watermelons are a classic fruit of summer. Sweet, refreshing, and perfect for picnics and barbecues, watermelons are a staple in many households during the warmer months.

However, have you ever wondered why some watermelons are sweeter, bigger, or even have more seeds than others? Believe it or not, the way you prune and thin your watermelon plant can have a significant impact on your harvest.

By removing excess growth and limiting the number of melons on each vine, you allow the plant to direct its energy toward producing larger and sweeter melons.

Proper pruning and thinning also reduce the risk of disease and pests, ensuring a healthy and bountiful harvest. So, next time you're tending to your watermelon patch, consider giving your plants a little trim to reap the benefits of juicy, delicious melons all summer long.

Pruning involves removing unwanted shoots, runners, and leaves that may inhibit watermelon growth and cause nutrient competition.

Thinning, on the other hand, requires removing some of the developing fruits to ensure the remaining fruits reach their maximum size and flavor potential. Timing is crucial, and knowing when to make these cuts can make all the difference.

The best time to start pruning and thinning your watermelons is when the plants begin to vine and show signs of growth. Use sharp, clean shears to cut away any dead or diseased leaves, as well as any shoots that sprout from the base of the plant.

Be sure to also thin out the smaller, weaker watermelons to give the more prominent one's room to grow. With these simple tips, your watermelon patch is sure to be bountiful and sweet.

Watering Watermelon's

Watermelons are a delicious summer fruit that can quench your thirst and satisfy your sweet tooth, but did you know how you water them can make all the difference in their growth and flavor?

Watering your watermelons correctly is crucial to their development, as they need consistent moisture throughout their growing season. Giving them too little or too much water can lead to a host of problems, such as cracked fruit, stunted growth, and disease.

By taking the time to water your Watermelons correctly, you can ensure their tastiness and abundance and, most importantly, give them the love and care they need to thrive.

If you're looking to grow some tasty watermelons, you'll need to make sure they're getting enough water. But how much is enough? And how often should you be watering them?

First, it's essential to ensure you're giving your watermelons a deep watering once a week rather than a light watering every day. This will help encourage deeper root growth and stronger plants.

You'll also want to make sure the soil is moist but not waterlogged, as too much water can lead to rot or disease. Finally, pay attention to the weather and adjust your watering schedule accordingly - on hot or windy days, your watermelons may need more frequent watering to stay hydrated.

It's also worth noting that watermelons love warm soil, so try to avoid watering during the hottest part of the day.

Fertilization For Watermelon

Fertilization is a crucial component of watermelon cultivation that can make all the difference in the size, sweetness, and overall quality of the fruit.

When watermelon plants are fertilized, they can absorb the necessary nutrients to produce strong roots, stems, and leaves. As a result, they can better absorb water, which is vital for the development of juicy and sweet fruit.

Without proper fertilization, watermelon plants can struggle to produce the plump, delicious fruit we all know and love. In short, fertilization is the key to growing delicious and healthy watermelons that everyone can enjoy.

So, the next time you bite into a juicy watermelon, remember that it's thanks to the fertilization process that you can enjoy this summertime treat.

One of the most important factors when it comes to watermelon cultivation is using the right fertilizer at the right time. For optimum growth and flavor, it is recommended to use a balanced fertilizer that contains nitrogen, phosphorus, and potassium NPK 10-10-10.

Applying the fertilizer before planting will help provide nutrients for the seedlings as they grow and again once the plants have started producing fruit. However, be careful not to over-fertilize, as this can lead to overly bushy plants with small fruit.

Using organic fertilizers is a great approach to nurturing your watermelon plants. Organic fertilizers like compost, manure, bone meal, and fish emulsion provide the essential nutrients that watermelons need for healthy growth.

Compost is rich in nitrogen, phosphorus, and potassium, which help in enhancing soil quality. Manure is also a great source of nutrients like nitrogen, potassium, and phosphorus, and it also increases soil fertility. Bone meal provides a natural source of phosphorus, while fish emulsion adds extra nitrogen, phosphorus, and potassium.

Using organic fertilizers not only promotes healthy plant growth but also reduces the risk of chemical contamination that can endanger the environment and your health.

PROTECTING YOUR WATERMELONS

Extreme Temperatures

Watermelons are a delicious summertime treat, but extreme temperatures can damper their sweet potential. Whether you're a seasoned watermelon grower or just starting out, it's important to take steps to protect your prized fruits from unpredictable weather patterns.

The key to safeguarding your crop against extreme temperatures is to plan ahead and be proactive in your approach. Consider using shade cloth or row covers to shield your watermelons from direct sunlight during the hottest part of the day.

Additionally, maintaining adequate moisture levels in your soil can help regulate temperature fluctuations and prevent your watermelons from becoming stressed or damaged. With a bit of extra care and attention, you can enjoy juicy, ripe watermelons all season long.

Protecting Watermelon From Pest

Watermelons are a summertime staple, but unfortunately, pests love them just as much as we do. Protecting watermelons from pests is a task that requires careful planning and attention to detail.

One of the keys to success is identifying the type of pests and taking the necessary precautions to keep them at bay.

Aphids, spider mites, and cucumber beetles are among the most common pests that attack watermelons.

These insects can cause severe damage to the fruit and its vines, ultimately reducing the harvest. These tiny insects not only feast on the foliage, but they also transmit disease to the watermelon plant.

To prevent these pests from ruining your watermelon harvest, consider using row covers or planting trap crops. Further prevention methods such as crop rotation, selecting resistant seed varieties, and proper garden sanitation, keeping your garden clean and free of debris can avoid infestations in the first place.

Additionally, companion planting is an eco-friendly way to deter pests. Planting herbs like basil, mint, or marigolds alongside your watermelons can repel insects and promote healthy growth.

Another option is to use insecticidal soap or neem oil, which are natural and safe alternatives to traditional pesticides. By taking measures to safeguard your watermelons, you can ensure a bountiful and delicious harvest all season long.

HARVESTING WATERMELON'S

When it comes to growing watermelons, the waiting game is real. Harvest time can vary depending on several factors, such as the type of watermelon, climate, and growing conditions.

However, watermelons generally take anywhere from 70 to 100 days to mature and ready for harvest. It's important to keep an eye on them during this time, checking for signs of ripeness, such as a change in color and a dull sound when tapped.

Patience is definitely key when it comes to harvesting these juicy fruits, but the payoff speaks for itself.

Harvesting watermelon fruits is rewarding and fun - however, not everyone knows how to properly harvest this refreshing fruit. First and foremost, it's important to wait until the fruit is fully ripe.

To determine this, look for a yellow or cream-colored spot on the underside where the fruit has been resting on the ground. Use a sharp knife or shear to cut the stem, leaving a short nub.

Do not pull the watermelon, as this can cause damage. To ensure even ripening, you can also rotate the watermelon every few days. With these simple steps, you can easily harvest your watermelon fruits and enjoy their sweet and juicy taste.

SAVING WATERMELON SEEDS

Harvesting your watermelon seeds is not only a great way to save money on your next crop but also allows you to enjoy the delicious flavor season after season.

To begin, start by selecting a mature watermelon that is fully ripe. Next, carefully cut it open with a sharp knife and scoop out the juicy flesh. Rinse the seeds in a colander and allow them to dry on a clean towel for a few hours.

Once dry, transfer the seeds to an airtight container, such as a mason jar, and store them in a cool, dry place. When you're ready to enjoy them, add some salt and roast them in the oven for a crunchy, flavorful snack.

Whether you plan to eat the seeds as a healthy snack, for future cultivation, or use them in a recipe, storing them correctly will ensure that you get the most out of this often-overlooked part of the watermelon.

CHAPTER 8
GROWING YOUR SUMMER ORANGES

There are many reasons to start your own orange garden beyond just the satisfaction of fresh produce in your backyard. For starters, growing your own oranges means you'll have access to the freshest, most flavorful fruit possible - one that hasn't been sitting in a warehouse or on a truck for weeks.

Plus, it can be a great way to save money on buying oranges from the store, especially if you have a large family or love to use oranges in cooking and baking. Summer oranges are packed with vitamin C, making them an excellent choice for boosting your immune system during the hotter months. Plus, tending to your own tree is a fun and rewarding activity that can involve the whole family.

So why not give it a try. With some patience and know-how, you'll soon be enjoying the fruits of your labor.

THE RIGHT SOIL FOR ORANGES

When cultivating oranges, testing the soil is a crucial step that shouldn't be overlooked. Our soil is the foundation of our crops, and by determining its nutrient content, pH levels, and other key factors, we can ensure optimal growth and fruit quality.

By neglecting this important aspect of farming, we run the risk of stunted growth, low yields, and even disease within our orchards. Taking the time to test our soil beforehand is a wise investment and a responsible decision that will ultimately lead to a more bountiful and healthier harvest.

So, if you're planning to cultivate oranges or any other type of produce, don't skip this essential process. Your crops will thank you for it.

The best soil for growing summer oranges is well-draining, slightly acidic soil with a pH between 6.0 and 6.5. Summer oranges thrive in soil rich in nutrients, so adding organic matter such as compost or aged manure can give the trees an extra boost.

While some soils can contribute to the growth and health of orange trees, others can have quite the opposite effect. It is best to avoid grounds that are heavy in clay or sand, as these types of soil can cause waterlogging or drought.

Orange Plant Diseases

As beautiful as orange plants arc, they are not immune to diseases. There are several types of diseases that affect these plants, but the most common ones include leaf spot, root rot, and powdery mildew.

Leaf spot appears as brown or black spots on the leaves, while root rot mainly affects the plant's roots, turning them brown and mushy. Powdery mildew, on the other hand, appears as white powder on the leaves. To prevent these diseases from spreading, it is key to undertake regular plant maintenance practices such as pruning, mulching, and watering.

Additionally, you can protect the plants from pests by ensuring you keep a clean environment - picking up dropped leaves or fruits. Avoid over-fertilizing your plants and handle them with care, especially during transplanting. With proper preventive measures, you can enjoy a thriving and healthy orange plant all year round.

When it comes to gardening, it's crucial to know which plants can grow harmoniously alongside each other. Orange trees, for example, may seem like a fantastic addition to your garden, but it's essential to know which plants you should avoid planting around them.

One such plant to avoid is the potato. This may surprise many, but the potato plant releases a toxin called solanine, which can harm the orange tree's roots, leading to stunted growth and decreased fruit yield. Plants such as alfalfa and clover release chemicals that inhibit the growth of orange trees.

Additionally, plants like tomatoes and peppers are hosts for insects that can cause damage to orange trees. Researching and avoiding planting these types of plants around your orange trees is essential to ensure their health and longevity.

If you want to create a thriving and diverse orchard in your backyard, consider planting companion fruit plants around your orange trees. This technique involves selecting various plants that can provide benefits to your orange trees, such as attracting beneficial insects or adding nutrients to the soil.

For example, strawberries make great companions for orange trees because they have shallow roots and won't compete for nutrients while attracting pollinators. Blueberries and blackberries are also great options, as they prefer the same acidic soil as oranges and can help maintain soil moisture.

Additionally, consider planting lemon trees around your orange tree. Not only do these two fruits complement each other beautifully in flavor, but lemon trees also provide an added touch of fragrance to your garden.

With some careful planning and selection, planting companion fruit plants can enhance the health and productivity of your orange trees while creating a beautiful and vibrant ecosystem in your backyard.

HOW TO SOW ORANGES

Correct Season to Sow Oranges

Oranges are a beloved fruit known for their tangy flavor and bright orange color. While they can be found in some grocery stores year-round, those who want to grow their own oranges need to pay attention to the right season.

Luckily, there is a clear answer to the question of when to grow oranges. In short, winter is the ideal time to plant orange seeds, with January through March as the best months for planting. During this period, the temperature is lower, providing the ideal conditions for oranges to ripen and reach their full flavor potential.

This timing allows the oranges to grow and thrive during the spring and summer months. So, if you're looking to grow your oranges, make sure to plan and plant accordingly.

Plant Needs and Requirements

Growing orange trees from seeds can be a rewarding and fulfilling experience. However, it is essential to follow the proper steps to ensure that the trees yield a bountiful harvest. To get started, begin by selecting seeds that are fresh and viable.

Next, soak the seeds in warm water for 24 hours to help soften the tough outer layer. Once you have your seeds, prepare a pot with high-quality soil and plant your seed around one inch deep.

Keep the soil moist but not overly saturated and place the pot in a sunny area where it can receive at least six hours of sunlight per day. Regular watering and fertilization will also ensure your orange trees grow strong and healthy.

If you're looking to grow your own oranges from seeds, it's important to understand the ideal conditions for germinating the seeds. One key factor is temperature - after all, seeds won't sprout if they aren't in a suitable environment.

The optimal temperatures for orange seeds to germinate are between 68-85 degrees Fahrenheit. These temperatures are dependent on a number of factors, including humidity and lighting conditions. Understanding the best conditions for germination can be key to growing healthy orange trees.

Orange seedlings are a fascinating phenomenon in their own right. These young sprouts hold the potential that one day they might grow into towering, fruit-bearing trees.

However, as with all things in life, they need the proper nurturing to realize their full potential. So, when is the right time to transplant them? Typically, orange seedlings are ready to be transplanted when they have grown at least six inches tall and developed a solid root system.

It's important to monitor the soil moisture and provide plenty of sunlight so the seedlings can grow strong and healthy. The orange seedlings should be transplanted carefully, ensuring not to damage the roots or disturb the delicate balance of the plant's ecosystem.

Spacing and Measurement

When it comes to transplanting orange seedlings, spacing, and measurements should not be taken lightly. The proper placement and measurement of each seedling can mean the difference between a healthy, fruitful orange tree and a struggling one.

It's important to remember that these young plants need enough space to spread their roots and absorb the necessary nutrients. In addition, paying close attention to the measurements will prevent overcrowding which can lead to disease, and provide enough air circulation for the orange seedlings to thrive.

With the right spacing and measurements, your orange trees have a better chance of growing strong and producing bountiful fruit.

Planting orange seedlings is more than digging a hole and dropping them in. Orange seedlings should be planted about 18-22 feet apart in rows spaced 20-25 feet apart.

The depth of the planting hole should be roughly the same depth as the container they came in. Remember, the goal here is to provide the seedlings with optimal conditions to bear healthy and delicious fruit in the coming years. By following these guidelines, you'll be well on your way to planting a thriving orange grove.

MAINTAINING YOUR ORANGES

Maintaining your orange trees is crucial if you want to enjoy their sweet and juicy fruits for many years to come. Proper care and attention not only ensure the tree's health and longevity but also guarantee high-quality yields.

Regular pruning and fertilizing can help you keep pests and diseases at bay, while regular watering and monitoring soil conditions can help you avoid drought and soil depletion.

Additionally, maintaining your orange trees can also create an aesthetically pleasing landscape that adds value to your property. Ultimately, investing time and effort in caring for your orange trees is a wise decision that yields both tangible and intangible benefits.

Pruning and Thinning Your Orange Trees

Pruning and thinning your orange trees may seem tedious, but it can make a world of difference in your tree's overall health and productivity.

By removing dead or diseased wood, you provide good ventilation and sun exposure to the remaining branches. This helps prevent disease and allows your tree to produce larger, juicier oranges.

Thinning out overly dense areas of the tree can promote better air circulation and allow for better fruit growth. Not to mention, by maintaining the shape of your tree with regular pruning, you can also create a more beautiful and visually appealing addition to your backyard.

By regularly pruning and thinning your orange tree, you improve its appearance and promote its overall health, ensuring you can enjoy the sweet, tangy taste of oranges for years to come.

Timing is critical when pruning your trees, with late winter and early spring being the ideal time to get started. But don't just start cutting away randomly - it's important to have a plan and know which branches to remove.

Focus on removing dead, diseased, or damaged branches first, then move on to thinning out congested areas to allow for better airflow and sun exposure. With a bit of careful attention and knowledge, your orange tree will thrive and produce delicious fruit for years to come.

Watering Oranges

Orange trees are a beautiful and productive addition to any garden or orchard. However, it is essential to water them correctly to ensure that they bear healthy and ripe fruit.

Many people make the mistake of under or over-watering their orange trees, causing them to suffer and eventually die. Orange trees need regular watering, but not too much or too little. Adequate watering helps the trees absorb nutrients from the soil, which is critical for their growth and fruit production.

By watering your orange trees correctly, you will ensure their health and longevity and enjoy a bountiful harvest of delicious oranges.

To ensure your orange trees get the right amount of water, you need to consider factors like the soil type, temperature, and humidity. So how do you strike the perfect balance?

The secret is to water deeply and infrequently, allowing the soil to dry out slightly before the next watering. Regularly checking the soil moisture level and adjusting your watering schedule is vital to keeping your orange trees happy and healthy.

A good rule of thumb is to apply enough water to moisten the soil to a depth of 2 to 3 feet. This typically means watering until you see it pooling, then stopping and allowing it to soak in. Water at the tree's base, avoiding spraying the leaves - this will encourage the roots to grow deeper, making the tree more drought-tolerant.

Fertilization For Oranges

Fertilization is an essential aspect of growing healthy and fruitful orange trees. Fertilizer provides trees with the vital nutrients they need to thrive, such as nitrogen, phosphorus, and potassium.

These nutrients are responsible for important processes like photosynthesis and cell division, which, in turn, support the growth of the tree and its fruit.

Without an adequate supply of nutrients, orange fruit trees can become weak and vulnerable to diseases or pest attacks. Furthermore, inadequate fertilization can lead to poor fruit quality, such as smaller or misshapen fruits with lower sugar content.

Proper fertilization also ensures that orange trees are less susceptible to diseases and pests, making them more resilient in harsh weather conditions. So, it is essential to fertilize orange trees regularly to ensure their optimal growth, health, and fruitful yield.

Choosing the right fertilizer is crucial to ensure your orange trees thrive and produce high-quality fruit. A balanced fertilizer with equal nitrogen, phosphorus, and potassium is ideal for orange trees.

However, looking for fertilizers specifically formulated for citrus plants is also smart. As for timing, it's recommended to fertilize your orange trees during the spring and summer months, as this is when they are in their active growth phase.

For orange trees, organic fertilizers such as compost, bone meal, blood meal, and fish emulsion can also be used.

Compost is a mixture of organic matter that enriches the soil with nutrients and improves soil structure.

Bone meal is high in phosphorus, which helps in the growth of new roots and fruit development.

Blood meal is rich in nitrogen, which stimulates leaf and stems growth.

Lastly, fish emulsion is an excellent source of nitrogen, phosphorus, and potassium, which promotes healthy plant growth and development.

By incorporating the right fertilizer at the right time, you'll be well on your way to enjoying a bountiful harvest of sweet, succulent oranges in no time.

PROTECTING YOUR ORANGES

Extreme Temperatures

As enjoyable as it is to see your orange fruit trees thrive, it can be devastating to watch them suffer from extreme temperatures. During hot summers or cold winters, it's important to take steps to protect your trees and ensure a healthy crop.

Fortunately, there are several steps you can take to protect them. The first way to protect your orange fruit trees is by mulching. Mulching your trees with organic matter like compost or wood chips can help regulate soil temperature and prevent root damage.

One method is to provide shade during the hottest part of the day or cover the trees with a breathable fabric to prevent sun scorch. For cold weather, wrapping the trunk and lower branches with insulation can help prevent damage from freezing temperatures.

Lastly, providing your trees with proper irrigation is essential to ensure they stay hydrated and can handle temperature changes. Following these steps can help safeguard your orange fruit trees and enjoy healthy, thriving plants year-round.

Protecting Oranges From Pest

Orange plants are absolutely delightful, from their vibrant hue to their sweet and zesty taste, but pests can quickly turn any grower's dream of a bountiful crop into a nightmare.

Some of the most common pests that affect orange trees are leafminers. These pests burrow into the leaves and cause them to curl, diminishing the tree's ability to photosynthesize.

Another pesky intruder is the spider mite, which feeds on the tree's leaves and sucks their life out, eventually causing leaf drops.

The citrus whitefly, which feeds on the tree sap and can cause yellowing of the leaves and an overall decline in the tree's health. The citrus rust mite can cause small bumps on the fruit, making it unappealing for eating and selling.

The Mexican fruit fly and the Mediterranean fruit fly. These insects lay their eggs inside the fruit, and the larvae start burrowing and feeding on the juicy flesh, leaving an unsavory mess behind.

The citrus psyllid not only nibbles on leaves but also spreads the dreaded Huanglongbing (HLB) disease.

Thankfully, there are ways to discourage these pesky creatures from ever getting close. One effective method is to prune your tree regularly to remove any dead branches or leaves that may be attracting pests.

Additionally, using insecticidal soaps or oils can help to control and prevent the spread of pests. It's also essential to ensure the soil around the tree is well-draining to prevent soggy roots, which can weaken the tree and make it more vulnerable to pest infestations. Another option is to apply sticky traps that capture the insects before they can reach the precious fruit.

Finally, monitor your tree regularly for signs of damage and act promptly if you notice any issues. With these measures in place, your orange fruit tree will be well protected from the pesky critters that would love to snack on your sweet, juicy oranges.

HARVESTING ORANGES

Orange fruit trees are a treasured addition to many gardens and orchards. With their beautiful bright oranges and sweet flavor, it's no wonder why people love to culti-vate these trees.

However, many people wonder just how long it takes for the fruit to be ready to harvest. Well, the answer to that question is not a simple one.

The time it takes for an orange fruit tree to mature and grow fruit can vary depending on several factors. These factors can include the type of orange tree, the climate of the region, the care that the tree receives, and soil quality.

That being said, most orange fruit trees take anywhere from 2 to 4 years to start bearing fruit and can continue to produce for up to 25 years or more. So although it may take a bit of patience, the reward of a bountiful orange harvest is well worth the wait.

Harvesting orange fruit trees can be a rewarding process that invites you to savor the sweet and juicy fruits of your labor. Whether you're growing oranges for personal consumption or for larger-scale distribution, there are several steps involved in ensuring a successful harvest.

First, determine the ripeness of your oranges by examining their color and firmness. Make sure that the fruit is ripe by gently pressing on it. If it gives slightly, it is ready to be harvested.

If your oranges are still green, this is a clear indication that they are not ready to be harvested. A full vibrant orange color is precisely what you should be looking for.

Use pruning shears or a sharp knife to cut the stem close to the fruit, being careful not to damage or pull on the tree branches. Be sure to leave a small stem attached to the fruit, as this can prolong its shelf life.

It's also important to harvest the fruit as soon as possible to avoid over-ripening or spoiling. Once all the oranges have been picked, store them in a cool, dry place to keep them fresh. With a little patience and care, you can enjoy the sweet taste of fresh oranges straight from your own backyard.

SAVING ORANGE SEEDS

Have you ever wondered how to harvest orange seeds? Well, there are a few simple steps to follow. First, cut open the orange and remove the flesh. Then, place the seeds in a sieve and rinse them under running water to remove any remaining pulp. After cleaning them, lay the seeds out to dry completely.

Once completely dry, store them in an airtight container or small ziplock bag away from direct sunlight. Be sure to label the container with the date and type of seed for easy reference. With these simple steps, you can store your orange seeds for future use and enjoy the bounty they bring.

CHAPTER 9
GROWING YOUR SUMMER GRAPES

G rowing your own summer grapes can be a rewarding and delightful experience with many benefits. Not only do you get to enjoy the satisfaction of growing your own fruit, but it can also save you money in the long run.

Being able to pick your own fresh grapes straight from the vine means you have control over the quality and freshness of the produce. Additionally, grapes are packed with antioxidants, making them a nutritious addition to your diet.

Growing summer grapes can also be a fun and educational activity for the whole family, teaching children the importance of sustainability and self-sufficiency. Cultivating your own grapes means you have complete control over the fertilizers and pesticides used, ensuring that you and your family are consuming only the healthiest fruits possible.

Additionally, tending to your grapevines can be a relaxing and therapeutic activity, bringing you closer to nature and reducing stress.

Whether you plan to use them for snacking, making wine, or adding to your favorite recipes, growing your own summer grapes will certainly add a fresh twist to your summer harvest.

THE RIGHT SOIL FOR GRAPES

To ensure a thriving vineyard, it is essential to test your soil before planting grapes. Testing allows growers to understand the needs of their soil and tailor their cultivation methods to suit its unique requirements.

Each soil type has its own characteristics, including the pH level, nutrient content, and drainage. Without understanding these factors, grape growers risk planting in soil that may not support healthy vines, ultimately resulting in a smaller yield of lower-quality grapes.

Testing your soil can alleviate these concerns and lead to a successful harvest season. By taking the time to analyze your soil, you can give your vineyard the best possible opportunity for success.

For those looking to cultivate summer grapes, it's important to consider the right soil to yield a successful harvest. The ideal soil for growing grape vines should have good drainage and be well-aerated to allow for proper root growth.

In addition, the soil should be rich in nutrients such as nitrogen, phosphorus, and potassium, which are vital for healthy plant growth. When selecting soil for summer grapes, it's also important to consider the pH levels. Grapes prefer a pH level between 6.0 and 6.5, which is slightly acidic.

Two types of soils that should be avoided when growing grapes are sandy soil and heavy clay soil. Sandy soil doesn't hold onto water or nutrients well, which can leave grape vines thirsty and malnourished.

Heavy clay soil, on the other hand, can suffocate the roots of the grape vines due to its high compaction. It's important to choose soil that's well-draining, nutrient-rich, and not too compact for grape vines to thrive.

Grape Plant Diseases

Grapes are a delicious fruit enjoyed by many, but unfortunately, they are also susceptible to various diseases that can damage the vines and cause a lower-quality yield.

Fungal diseases like powdery mildew and downy mildew are common culprits, as well as viral diseases like leafroll disease. The good news is that preventing these diseases is possible, and it starts with practicing good vineyard management techniques.

One essential technique is pruning. By pruning the vines correctly, you can improve air circulation around the grape plants, which reduces the chances of disease spores settling on the plants.

Additionally, you should regularly inspect your vines for signs of disease and immediately remove any infected parts to prevent the spread.

Another critical step is to ensure your plants are getting enough water, light, and nutrients to help them stay healthy and resistant to diseases. Also, it is important to choose disease-resistant grape varieties when planting new vines. Remember that prevention is always better than cure, and by practicing good vineyard management techniques, you can go a long way in keeping your grape plants healthy and disease-free.

It's important to also consider what plants to avoid planting near your grapevines to ensure a healthy and thriving harvest. For instance, plants of the Brassica family, like broccoli or cabbage, should be kept clear of grapevines as they can attract pests and insects that can cause harm to the grape crop.

Additionally, plants that require heavy watering or nutrient-rich soil, such as roses or corn, can compete for nutrients and water, ultimately affecting the growth and development of the grapes.

Companion plants can have a significant impact on the overall health and growth of your grape vines. Luckily, there are several fruit plants that make great companions for grapevines.

One great option is blueberries, as they thrive in slightly acidic soil, just like grapes. Additionally, blueberries and grapes have similar water requirements, making it easy to keep them both hydrated as well as help to deter pests and protect your grapes from fungal diseases. Another great choice is strawberries. Not only do they add a pop of color to your garden, but they also attract pollinators that can benefit your grape vines.

HOW TO SOW GRAPES

Correct Season to Sow Grapes

Growing grapes is a popular pastime for many individuals, whether they are looking to make homemade wine or simply enjoy the sweet fruit fresh off the vine. When it comes to the perfect season for grape cultivation, there are a few important factors to consider. Planting a grapevine too early or too late can result in stunted growth, fewer grapes, or an unripe harvest.

Firstly, grapes thrive in warm, sunny weather, so it's important to plant them in the spring after the danger of frost has passed. This will give the vine enough time to establish roots before the hot summer months, which are essential for the fruit to mature.

Plant Needs and Requirements

Growing your own grapes from seeds can be a rewarding and satisfying experience. However, it's important to remember that this process takes time, patience, and a little bit of know-how. The first step is to choose the right grape variety and gather the necessary materials, such as good-quality soil, pots, and fertilizer.

Then, soak your grape seeds in water overnight, as this can help soften the seed coat and make germination easier. Next, plant the seeds about 1 inch deep and keep them moist. It's important to keep the right temperature and humidity for the seeds to sprout.

Temperature ranging between 70 and 80 degrees Fahrenheit is ideal - however, consider using a grow light if the climate is not fitting.

When it comes to transplanting grape seedlings, timing is everything. Determining when a seedling is ready for transplantation requires attention to details such as the plant's growth rate, root development, and environmental factors such as temperature and humidity.

It is important to note that grape seedlings have their own unique growth patterns and may take up to several weeks to reach maturity. In general, grape seedlings should be transplanted when they have grown several sets of true leaves, grown to a height of about six inches, and their roots have filled their containers.

With proper care and attention, these young plants will have a strong start in their new location and thrive for years to come.

Spacing and Measurement

When it comes to transplanting grape seedlings, spacing, and measurements are crucial elements to keep in mind. The process requires precision and attention to detail in order to ensure the healthy growth and development of the young plants. Proper spacing allows for adequate access to sunlight, air circulation, and necessary nutrients, all of which are important for optimal plant growth.

Additionally, precise measurements ensure that each seedling has enough room to grow without competing with neighboring plants. Neglecting these factors can result in stunted growth, weak plants, and, ultimately, disappointing harvests. Taking the time to carefully plan and execute the transplanting process can make all the difference in the success of your grape vineyard.

To determine the ideal spacing for your grape seedlings, consider the variety you are growing and the type of trellis or support system you will be using. The general rule of thumb is to space seedlings 6-8 feet apart in rows that are 8-10 feet apart.

It's also important to plant them at the same depth as they were in their previous container and to provide ample drainage and sunlight. This will allow the roots to establish themselves and the vines to grow strong and healthy.

Remember, the right spacing and measurements may vary depending on the grape variety and the climate you're planting in, so be sure to do your research beforehand. Additionally, plant them in a spot that receives at least 6 hours of direct sunlight daily.

Taking the time to research the optimal spacing and measurements for the grape variety you're growing will go a long way in guaranteeing a bountiful harvest.

MAINTAINING YOUR GRAPES

Maintaining your grape trees is incredibly important for several reasons. Firstly, proper upkeep ensures that you'll have a fruitful harvest. Without taking care of your trees, you may have a decreased yield or even a failed crop. Secondly, keeping your grape trees in good condition can help prevent disease and other issues that can affect the quality of your grapes.

Regular pruning and pest control measures can prevent the spread of disease and ensure that your grapes remain healthy and delicious. Finally, maintaining your grape trees shows you take pride in your work and care about your craft. It's a way to show respect for the land and for the fruits of your labor.

Proper maintenance will not only improve the quality and yield of your grapes but will also extend the lifespan of your grape trees for years to come. So don't overlook the importance of taking care of your grape trees, and enjoy the delicious fruits of your labor.

Pruning and Thinning Your Grape Vines

Pruning and thinning your grape vines may seem like tedious tasks, but they are crucial for maintaining a healthy and productive vineyard. By removing excess growth and limiting the number of clusters on each vine, you not only improve the quality of your grapes but also prevent disease and improve air circulation.

Without proper pruning and thinning, your grape vines can become overcrowded and unmanageable, leading to a decrease in yield and a lower-quality product. Don't over-look this important aspect of grape growing - take the time to carefully prune and thin your vines, and your hard work will pay off in delicious, healthy fruit.

The ideal time to prune is in late winter or early spring, while the vines are still dormant. During this time, you'll have a better idea of which buds are healthy and which ones need to go. This will ultimately encourage strong and vigorous growth for the upcoming season.

When pruning, make sure to get rid of any dead or diseased wood, as well as any growth that's not needed for the vine's structure.As for thinning, you'll want to wait until your grapes are starting to grow. This usually takes place during the summer months, and it involves removing some of the grape clusters to allow better airflow and sun exposure for the remaining grapes.

By properly pruning and thinning your grape vines, you'll have a healthier vineyard with a better chance of producing delicious fruit year after year.

Watering Grapes

Grapes are a delicate fruit that requires careful attention when it comes to watering. It's important to note that the amount of water they receive can significantly affect their growth and overall health.

Over-watering can lead to root rot or fungal diseases, while under-watering can result in stunted growth and poor-quality fruit. To ensure that your grape vines are thriving, it's essential to water them correctly.

This means giving them deep soakings at the roots, rather than just spraying them from above, and making sure that the soil is moist but not overly saturated. Proper watering supports healthy growth and can even improve the taste of your grape crop.

Grape vines are quite an investment, so it's important to ensure they get the right amount of water. First off, make sure that the soil around the vines is properly drained so that it doesn't become waterlogged.

Once you've done that, you can start watering your vines. Keep in mind that grape vines generally require a moderate amount of water—around 1-2 inches per week, depending on the climate and the type of vines you have. During periods of extended drought or heat, you may need to water your vines more frequently.

One way to check if your vines need water is to dig down a few inches and see if the soil feels dry. If it does, it's time to water your vines. Don't forget to also water the root zone around the vines, as this is where they'll be absorbing moisture from.

Mulching around the base of the plants can help retain moisture and keep weeds at bay. Additionally, watering early in the morning or late in the afternoon can help prevent evaporation and ensure the water is fully absorbed by the plants.

Fertilization For Grapes

Fertilization is a crucial aspect of grapevine cultivation, and not just because it promotes bud growth and enhances fruit production. It also helps to bolster the vine's overall health and strengthen its defenses against pests and disease.

Properly fertilized grapevines are more resistant to environmental stresses such as drought and extreme temperatures, which can impact both the yield and quality of the fruit. In fact, various studies have shown that properly fertilized vines produce more flavorful and aromatic grapes, leading to wines of superior quality.

So, while it may seem like a small piece of the puzzle, ensuring that grapevines receive adequate fertilization is a vital step in achieving the best possible results.

As most gardeners know, fertilizer is key to a healthy, bountiful harvest. But with so many options on the market, it can be overwhelming to know which type to use and when. The good news is that it's not as complicated as it seems.

The general rule is to fertilize your grape vines in early spring before bud break and then again in early summer when the fruit is developing, applying fertilizer at the right time can enhance the absorption and utilization of nutrients.

The type of fertilizer you use will depend on the needs of your soil and grape variety, but most grape vines benefit from a balanced blend of nitrogen, phosphorus, and potassium.

Organic grape production has been gaining popularity in recent years due to growing consumer demand for environmentally friendly farming practices. Fortunately, there are many types of organic fertilizers available that can improve grapevine growth and yield without the use of synthetic chemicals.

Common examples include compost, manure, seaweed, and bone meal. Each of these fertilizers has specific benefits - compost, and manure provide the soil with nutrition and help it retain moisture, seaweed adds beneficial micronutrients, and bone meal offers a slow-release source of phosphorus.

By using organic fertilizers, you can keep your grapevines healthy and productive while also being mindful of the environment.

PROTECTING YOUR GRAPES

Extreme Temperatures

As a grape grower, protecting your grape vines from extreme temperatures is crucial to ensure optimum grape production. Extreme temperatures can take a toll on your vines, causing them to be more susceptible to disease or even dying off entirely.

One strategy for protecting your vines is to provide ample protection during the winter months. Covering your vines with mulch or burlap can help protect them from freezing temperatures. Another strategy is to use irrigation to help regulate temperature, especially during the hot summer months.

Remember, protecting your grape vines requires diligence and care, but the rewards are worth it resulting to a healthy vineyard and bountiful harvests for years to come.

Protecting Grapes From Pest

Grape vines are a delicate crop that requires careful attention and monitoring to ensure a healthy harvest. One of the biggest threats to grape vines is pests, which can ruin the fruit and damage the vines themselves.

Common pests that attack grape vines include grape berry moths, spider mites, mealybugs, Japanese beetles, and aphids. These pests can damage the leaves, reducing the plant's ability to carry out photosynthesis and destroying the fruit, making it unfit for consumption.

Fortunately, there are several measures that one can take to prevent pest infestations on grape vines. One of the most effective ways to do this is by using natural methods like companion planting, crop rotation, and planting pest-resistant varieties.

Additionally, using organic sprays made from natural ingredients such as garlic, neem oil, or vinegar can deter pests from attacking your vines. Another effective method is to encourage beneficial insects such as ladybugs and praying mantis into the vineyard to naturally control pests.

It's important to monitor your grape vines regularly for signs of pests and take action as soon as you notice anything suspicious. Additionally, maintaining a clean and healthy environment around your vines by pulling out weeds and fallen fruit can also help prevent pests from nesting in and around your vineyard.

By taking these measures, not only will growers ensure a healthy harvest, but they will also help maintain a healthy ecosystem by avoiding the unnecessary use of harmful chemicals.

HARVESTING GRAPES

Grapes are one of the most popular and versatile fruits in the world. From wine-making to snacking, these little round fruits have a lot to offer. But have you ever wondered how long it takes for grapes to be ready for harvest? Well, the answer depends on a few factors. First, the variety of grapes plays a big role in determining the harvest time.

Some varieties mature faster than others. Second, the climate and weather conditions in the grape-growing region also play a role. Finally, the cultivation method being used can affect the harvest timing. Despite these variables, on average, grapes take around 100-120 days from bloom to harvest.

Harvesting grape vines is an important step for anyone cultivating grapes. Before starting the process, it's crucial to understand that the timing and technique involved in harvesting can affect the quality and taste of the grapes.

To start, it's important to keep a close eye on the grapes as they begin to ripen. This means checking the sugar levels and color of the grapes, as well as tasting them to ensure that they are sweet and juicy. A small handheld tool known as a refractometer can be used to test and verify the sugar levels of your grapes.

Depending on the variety of the grape you are growing, it is recommended to carry out additional research on the desired sugar levels of that variety.

Once the grapes have reached their peak ripeness, it's time to begin the harvest. Starting from the bottom of the vine, carefully cut off the clusters of grapes, being mindful not to damage the stems or grapes.

Pay attention to the color and taste of the grapes to determine when they are ready to be harvested. Be sure to use sharp and clean shears and place the grapes in containers that allow for proper ventilation.

With careful planning and execution, harvesting grape vines can be a rewarding process that produces high-quality fruit perfect for making wine or simply enjoying a delicious snack.

SAVING GRAPES SEEDS

Harvesting grape seeds can be a fun and rewarding experience for those who love gardening and winemaking. To begin, it's important to select mature grapes, which are dark in color and have a sweet aroma.

Once you have harvested the grapes, remove them from the stems and place them in a colander to wash off any debris. Next, gently squeeze the grapes to extract their pulp and seeds.

Separating the seeds from the pulp can be a bit tedious, but the end result is worth the effort. To do this, soak the pulp and seeds in water for a few hours, then strain the mixture through a fine mesh sieve. The seeds will remain behind, where you can dry them before storing or planting them.

Grape seeds can be a great addition to your pantry for baking, snacking, or adding to teas. However, if you don't store them properly, they can easily go stale and lose their flavor.

To keep your grape seeds fresh, it is recommended to store them in an airtight container away from heat and moisture. This will help to preserve their natural oils and prevent oxidation.

Another tip is to label the container with the date when you first stored the seeds, so you can keep track of their age. By following these simple steps, you can enjoy the rich nutty flavor of grape seeds in your recipes or for future cultivation.

CHAPTER 10
FRUIT SALAD RECIPES

Making your own fruit salad has numerous benefits that not only enhance your overall health but also appeal to your taste buds. One of the primary advantages is that you can customize the mix of fruits according to your preference and dietary needs. Plus, you get to experiment with different fruit combinations and explore new flavors.

Secondly, homemade fruit salads are fresher compared to store-bought options, as a result they retain a significant chunk of their essential nutrients. By creating your fruit salad using homemade fruits, you eliminate any unnecessary chemicals or preservatives, ensuring that your fruit salad is truly fresh and natural.

To ensure that your fruit salad is filled with the right mix of flavors and textures, you'll need a few essential tools. First, a good knife is crucial for cutting and preparing the fruits. A cutting board to protect your surfaces is also a must. For mixing all the ingredients together, a large bowl is highly recommended.

Don't forget a spoon or spatula for stirring. A citrus juicer can also come in handy if you plan on using any acidic fruits like oranges or lemons.

Now, to make a delicious fruit salad, start by selecting a variety of fresh fruits such as berries, melons, and grapes.

Fortunately, in this guide, we've walked through each stage of how to successfully cultivate and harvest raspberries, pears, apples, strawberries, kiwis, watermelons, oranges, and grapes. So there's a variety of concoctions to try and flavors to experiment with.

First, wash and chop the fruits into bite-sized pieces and combine them in a large mixing bowl. For an extra burst of sweetness, consider adding a drizzle of honey or a splash of citrus juice.

For added crunch, sprinkle chopped nuts or granola on top. To really take your fruit salad to the next level, add some herbs like mint or basil for a burst of fresh flavor. Give the salad a gentle toss to ensure all the fruit is evenly coated, and serve chilled.

Creating your own fruit salad is the perfect way to cool down on a hot summer day or to add some brightness and color to your daily meals.

Don't be afraid to experiment with different fruit combinations and toppings to create your own perfect fruit salad recipe.

CHAPTER 11
FRUIT SMOOTHIES RECIPES

What could be more satisfying than enjoying a delicious fruit smoothie on a hot summer day? Growing your own fruits to use in those smoothies might just take it to the next level.

Not only do you get to enjoy the satisfaction of growing and harvesting your own fruits, but you also get the added benefit of knowing exactly what goes into your smoothie. No artificial flavors or preservatives, just pure, wholesome goodness.

It may sound like a long shot, where some could easily think they aren't making an impact, but by using home-grown fruits to create your smoothies, you're reducing the amount of carbon emissions needed to transport produce from across the world or the journey to local supermarkets.

Whether it's a quick breakfast on the go or a refreshing afternoon snack, a homemade fruit smoothie is a tasty way to enjoy the fruits of your labor.

When it comes to making a delicious and healthy fruit smoothie, there are a few tools you'll need to get your hands on first. Of course, you'll need the essential ingredients for your smoothie, such as frozen fruit or fresh fruit, yogurt or milk, and any sweeteners or flavorings you prefer.

But beyond that, you'll need a blender to properly mix and liquefy your ingredients. Most blenders will do the trick, but investing in a high-speed blender will ensure maximum smoothness in your final product.

Additionally, a sharp knife and cutting board will be helpful for chopping up any larger pieces of fruit. Finally, if you like your smoothies on the go, a travel cup or lid is a great way to take your delicious creation with you wherever you go. With these tools at your disposal, you'll be whipping up smoothies in no time.

To make a fruit smoothie, start with your favorite fruits. As previously mentioned, you can use fresh or frozen fruits, depending on what you have on hand.

Cut up your fruits and add it to your blender. Next, add a liquid base of your choice, such as almond milk, orange juice, coconut water, or even yogurt, to help blend everything together.

For those looking for some extra sweetness, you can include honey or agave syrup, and for those who would prefer an extra boost of nutrition, there's always the option to add some spinach or kale to your smoothie.

Finally, blend everything together until smooth, and enjoy. Making a fruit smoothie is a quick and easy way to add

some healthy fruits to your diet, and with so many variations to try, you'll never get bored.

CHAPTER 12
FRUIT JUICE RECIPES

There's something magical about growing your own fruits and transforming them into delicious fresh juice. Not only is it incredibly satisfying to sip on something you've created with your own two hands, but there are a myriad of benefits to making your own fruit juice with fruits you've grown.

For example fruits that are freshly picked and used immediately have more vitamins and minerals than store-bought options that have been sitting on a shelf for weeks which often contain added sugars and preservatives. Additionally, when creating fruit juices with your own fruits you'll be able to experiment with different fruit combinations and ratios to create your very own signature juice blend.

So the next time you find yourself craving a refreshing glass of juice, consider reaching for the fruits you've grown and experience the pure joy of sipping on your own home-made creation.

Making fresh fruit juice is an enjoyable way to get a healthy dose of vitamins and minerals. However, before diving into the process, it's essential to have the right tools on hand. To create a delicious glass of fruit juice, all you need are some key pieces of equipment.

A great start is a quality juicer, capable of pulverizing your choice of fruit into liquid gold. This tool is crucial as it ensures the fruit is broken down efficiently. For citrus fruits like oranges or grapefruits, you'll want to invest in a manual or electric juicer specifically designed for them.

A sharp knife is also essential, as you'll need to peel and chop your fruit into manageable pieces before juicing. Finally, a sturdy cutting board and a citrus reamer will further assist in the juicing process. With these tools at your disposal, making your own delicious and refreshing fruit juice at home is easier than ever.

To start the process of concocting your fruit juice, you'll need to pick your fruits - whether it's sweet strawberries, succulent watermelon, or tart oranges.

Get creative and mix and match your favorites. Next, wash and chop the fruit into small pieces and squeeze them using a juicer or blender. If you prefer a smoother texture, strain the juice through a sieve to remove any remaining pulp.

Add a splash of lemon or lime juice for some extra acidity, and sweeten with honey or sugar to your desired taste. Additionally, water or ice cubes can be added to form a smoother consistency.

Just like that, your very own homemade fruit juice is ready to be enjoyed. Sipping on this nutritious beverage tastes even better knowing you grew and made it with your own hands.

CHAPTER 13
GLOSSARY

Acidic

Something that forms or becomes acid and has a pH of less than 7.

Aeration

The act of circulating air through a garden, soil, and plants.

Aged manure

Old manure that has matured through a long period by letting it sit in a container.

Alkaline

Something that contains alkali and has a pH above 7.

Aphids

Tiny insects which consume the liquid plants produce, such as sap.

Antioxidants

A chemical that guards against free radical damage to cells.

Bacteria

A microorganism that causes disease and, at other times, improves the well-being of an organism.

Biodegradable

Something that can decompose into the soil and not harm the soil or other living organisms in it.

Bolting

When vegetable crops prematurely run to seed, it usually makes them unusable.

Blunt

Something that is not sharp but softer around its edges and unable to penetrate through something.

Blanch

A method for growing vegetables. A condition in which a plant's young shoots are covered to block light, preventing photosynthesis and chlorophyll production, leaving them pale in color.

Bulb

A plant's fruit or organ grows in the soil above its roots and is typically edible as a vegetable plant.

Bushy

Something that is overgrown or grows to be dense, big, and has lots of leaves.

Cabbage loopers

An insect or moth tends to be found crawling and laying eggs on cabbages. This insect is a cabbage pest that destroys crops.

Calcium carbonate

Insoluble chalk is natural and white. This is also called ground limestone.

Collar

A round object is used to cuff the base of a plant to protect it from pests such as worms and maggots.

Compaction

The compression of soil particles removes air pockets and hardens the soil. It is considered harmful when gardening and if you want to achieve successful results.

Companion planting

Planting two or more plants next to each other and is protective of each other to avoid disease and pests. It can improve harvest results and improve growth.

Compost

A combination of biodegradable plants, objects, or waste mixed with rotting and building up nutrients necessary to soil health and fertility.

Container garden

A garden of plants grown in a pot that holds soil.

Crop rotation

Planting various crops in succession on the same piece of land helps to improve soil health, maximize nutrients, and reduce pest and weed pressure. This practice is known as crop rotation.

Cutworms

A damaging and destructive moth larva is a vegetable pest found in soil and on plants.

Composition

The character of something's components or ingredients; the composition of a whole or mixture.

Cholesterol

A waxy, fatty substance that permeates all of your body's cells.

Drought

Drought is an extended period of unusually dry weather with insufficient rain.

Debris

Remains or objects in the soil, such as rocks and previously dead crops, need to be removed to maintain the health of your garden.

Drainage

The process by which liquids or water is expelled from something, such as soil.

Drilling tractor

A gardening sowing machine that drills holes into the ground and helps a gardener avoid manual soil drilling to plant his plants.

Ecosystem

Different biological organisms interact with each other to maintain an environment.

Evaporation

Water that turns into vapor.

Fertile soil

Soil that is healthy enough to give plants all nutrients they need to grow successfully until harvest.

Fertilization

Making soil fertile through the use of fertilizers.

Frost

Ice crystals can form on plants when temperatures are freezing or too cold.

Frost Cloth

It is a covering made of insulation positioned over plants, shrubs, trees, and crops to shield them from frost, wind, and chilly weather.

Fungus

Living organisms feed on other living organisms and create mold or discolored plants when present. They can destroy plants and cause disease.

Flavonoids

A collection of organic compounds with varying phenolic structures.

Germinate

When a plant starts to grow out of a shell and form shoots or leaves.

Harvest

A collection of mature and ripe plants and their fruit. It's when your plants have matured, and you collect them from their stems.

Heart rate

How fast or slow are your heartbeats. It's a number or calculation which determines the heart's speed.

Humus

Decomposed organic matter consists of soil and compost.

Hybrid seed

Seeds have been altered and are offspring of two different seed varieties of the same plant.

Inflammation

The body's immune system reacts to an allergen by inflaming the affected area.

Mesh

A material you lace over your garden plants that protects them from insects and pests.

Minerals

Substances are naturally occurring and are needed to produce fertile soil and healthy plants.

Moisture

Dampness is caused by diffused water or liquid.

Mulch

Decayed matter, such as compost, is placed on the soil's surface to lock moisture in or protect the soil from harsh weather conditions.

Nitrogen

A nutrient is needed to give plants their green color and healthy leaves.

Nutrients

Elements that feed plants the necessary food they need to grow.

Organic matter

Decomposed humus is in the soil and is essential in growing healthy vegetables.

Organic produce

Food that has been made or grown without the use of chemical alterations.

Pesticides

Organic or chemical substances kill or repel insects and other pests from a garden.

Pests

Living organisms are destructive to a garden and must be repelled or prevented from reaching plants.

pH

A chemistry figure which communicates a scale of alkalinity or acidity. It helps you know how alkaline or acidic soil is.

Phosphate

Phosphoric acid is a salt needed for the soil's health.

Potassium

It is a nutrient that helps plants grow and is essential in their life cycle.

Pruning

Maintain a garden by cutting or trimming dead or potentially unwanted plant parts.

Pollinating

The act of transferring pollen grains from the male anther of a flower to the female stigma.

Particles

A tiny amount of something.

Roots

The bottom stingy and firm bits of a plant grow and stretch into the soil. They absorb the nutrients and water for a plant's needs.

Sedimentary

A rock that was created from sediment that was carried by the wind or water.

Shrubs

A woody plant is smaller than a tree and typically has numerous persistent stems that sprout from the ground or nearby.

Seedling

A small and recently germinated plant that is ready to be planted.

Soggy

A mushy, soft, and overly damp area such as soil.

Soilless

Matter which seeds can be grown in and is an alternative to soil.

Sowing

The act of planting, drilling, or scattering a seed onto or into the soil to grow.

Sprout

When a plant produces its first shoots or leaves.

Stem

The structure of a plant that supports all its branches, leaves, and fruit.

Suckers

Plant suckers are vigorous vertical growth originating from a plant's root system or lower main stem.

Shoots

The portion of a plant that grows above ground and contains flowering buds, lateral buds, and flowering stems is called a shoot.

Substrate

The foundation upon or over which an organism lives or moves.

Substances

A specific type of substance with consistent qualities.

Thinning

Separating seedlings clumped together or removing some overcrowded plants from the soil to space out your garden to allow others to grow properly.

Transplanting

When you take a plant from one soil, area, or tray into another area or garden, this is also known as replanting it into another space.

Vitamins

Any of a set of chemical substances that are necessary for healthy development and nutrition and that must be consumed in small amounts in the diet because the body is unable to synthesize them.

ACKNOWLEDGEMENTS

Without the knowledge, experience, and commitment of our team at Green Roots, this book would not be possible. We appreciate your contributions to this book, Charles Craig, Annie Hayford, Jessica Reid, Adam Spencer, and Nicole Robinson. Your dedication to making a difference in people's lives and developing this community gardening is unmatched.

This book is the product of more than 20 years of collective expertise, experience, insight, and passion for gardening. We are all thrilled to have been able to create this body of work, to help, and to be used as a tool worldwide for gardeners of all levels of experience.

AFTERWORD

There is no denying the benefits of starting your own garden. It genuinely has the power to change your life in ways you could never have imagined. Your overall well-being can flourish, and your health can get better.

At Green Roots, we are confident in the transformative power of gardening, and the science backs it up. By engaging in this therapeutic hobby and pastime, you can experience significant improvements in your quality of life, both now and in the long run.

We have countless stories about how gardening has bene-fited us personally, and we have seen firsthand how it can impact the lives of others. Our work with various groups has allowed us to witness the immediate and long-term positive effects on people's lives. They feel better, have a more positive outlook, and are happier.

Gone are the days when you needed a big garden, fancy tools, and expensive equipment to grow your own fresh produce.

Unfortunately, many still believe this myth and find gardening intimidating. And while there are plenty of books promising to make gardening "easy," they often fall short. That's where this guide comes in.

We've taken on the challenge of dispelling these myths and simplifying the process. We want our readers to feel confident and equipped to take on any gardening challenge - don't worry about fancy jargon or sounding like an expert, we've written it all in plain English intending to make gardening easy to understand.

Yes, becoming an skilled gardener is wonderful, especially when you can share your knowledge with others. However, ensuring that your expertise is understandable and applicable is essential.

This practical guide covers everything you need to know about growing summer fruits as well as recipes for the freshest fruit salads, smoothies, and fruit juices.

Even better, the knowledge and tips included can easily be applied to many other fruits you decide to grow during this season, making this guide exceptionally timeless.

Whether you're a novice or a veteran gardener, this guide has got you covered. With the fundamental principles of gardening that remain unchanged, you can rely on this book for years to come.

This lifelong resource can always be referred to, even years from now, and you'll still have a firm grasp on how to grow and cultivate your plants.

Types of Gardens

Even if you don't have a large yard, you learned that you can still enjoy gardening. In this guide, you've learned that starting in containers is a great option to get started and improvise as necessary.

However, it's important to note that some plants may not thrive in containers due to their need for deep roots.

In this guide, you've learned and understood the three different types of gardens:

Container Gardens - A great option for those with limited space, but may not be suitable for all plants.

Raised Bed Gardens - An excellent choice for those with poor soil quality or limited mobility.

Traditional In-Ground Gardens - The classic way to cultivate fruits and vegetables with plenty of space and soil.

By the end of this guide, you will have a thorough understanding of the benefits and drawbacks of each gardening option. So don't wait any longer - start your garden today.

Preparing the Soil

As a new gardener, it can be easy to overlook the importance of soil when setting up your garden. Many beginners simply purchase compost and fertilizer without understanding their soil's type or needs. However, soil and fertility are critical to your plant's growth and yield.

By learning about your soil, you can prepare, improve, maintain, and protect it to ensure the best possible results. In this guide, we've covered everything you need to know about soil for your garden, so you can get started on the right foot.

Don't let your hard work go to waste - take the time to get to know your soil.

Deciding What to Grow

If you're a beginner gardener, it's easy to get excited and start planting seeds without much thought. But before you do, it's important to ask yourself - why are you starting a fruit garden?

This guide is designed to help you make informed decisions about the types of fruits you should grow based on your personal needs. After all, why spend time growing fruits that won't make a significant difference in your life?

By taking the time to consider your "why," you'll be able to choose the right fruits to plant while staying motivated throughout the growing process.

Keep in mind that your choice of fruits should be personal and meaningful to you and not driven by anyone else's unless you are gardening for a cause other than yourself.

With this guide, you'll be on your way to a bountiful and fulfilling fruit garden that aligns with your goals and priorities.

Sowing Techniques

In this guide you've discovered that sowing methods and techniques differ depending on the type of garden you want to plant and the size you want it to be.

This information provided reinforces your understanding of the techniques and why they would or would not work in your garden. Each sowing technique is unique, but they can all be used in various situations. This knowledge will assist you in avoiding time-consuming errors and worse financial loss due to incorrect sowing.

Growing Your Summer Fruits

The primary and most important points you've taken from this guide are found in each fruit guide for raspberries, pears, apples, strawberries, kiwis, watermelon, oranges, and grapes.

With the in-depth guidance provided on each fruit, you can now take actionable and confident steps from germinating your seeds all the way through to harvesting. As a result, you can expect the freshest and ripest fruits this summer.

The straightforward nature of this book, its advice, and its instructions will help any novice gardener thrive in cultivating a successful fruit garden. It will show you how simple gardening can be, how rewarding it can be, and how it can improve your life.

We truly hope you'll discover the joy and satisfaction that comes from cultivating a thriving, harmonious fruit garden and would love to share this experience with you via our Facebook gardening community - **facebook.-com/groups/greenroots/**

Now that you're well-equipped to start your summer fruit garden journey, we would appreciate if you could give an honest review of this guide. Your feedback and thoughts help us determine whether we did an excellent job of assisting you in improving your gardening skills. Feel free to post them in the comments and reviews section of your purchased retailer, and we'll keep an eye out for them.

"Garden is not just a hobby, but a way of life" - Green Roots

ALSO BY GREEN ROOTS

Fruit and Veggies 101 - Vegetable Companion Planting: Companion Guide On How To Grow Vegetables Using Essential, Organic & Sustainable Gardening Strategies

Fruit and Veggies 101

VEGETABLE COMPANION PLANTING

Companion Guide On How To Grow Vegetables Using Essential Organic & Sustainable Gardening Strategies

(Perfect For Beginners)

GREEN ROOTS

Fruit & Veggies 101 - Salad Vegetables: Gardening Guide On How To Grow the Freshest & Ripest Salad Vegetables (Perfect for Beginners)

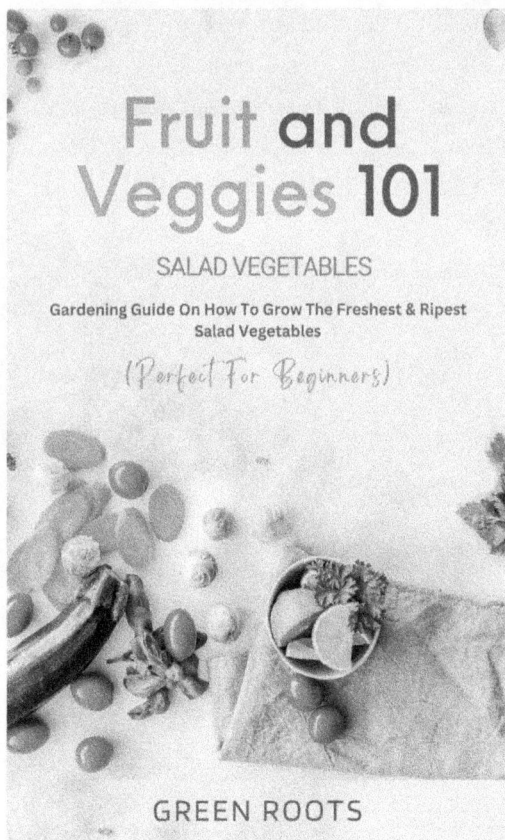

Fruit **and** Veggies **101**

SALAD VEGETABLES

Gardening Guide On How To Grow The Freshest & Ripest Salad Vegetables

(Perfect For Beginners)

GREEN ROOTS

Fruit & Veggies 101 - The Winter Harvest: Gardening Guide On How to Grow the Freshest & Ripest Winter Vegetables (Perfect for Beginners)

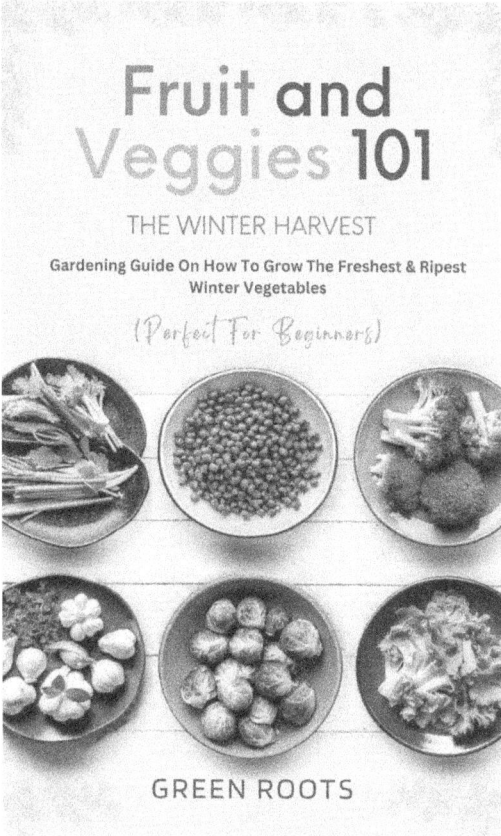

Fruit and Veggies 101

THE WINTER HARVEST

Gardening Guide On How To Grow The Freshest & Ripest Winter Vegetables

(Perfect For Beginners)

GREEN ROOTS

BIBLIOGRAPHY

10 Reasons to Grow Your Own Organic Food. (2016, February 2). Grow a Good Life. https://growagoodlife.com/grow-your-own-organic-food/

Andrew. (2020, April 23). What Tools Do I Need To Start a Vegetable Garden? - Gardening FAQs. Quickcrop Blog. https://www.quick-crop.co.uk/blog/what-tools-do-i-need-to-start-a-vegetable-garden/

Asher, B. (2011). What Is the Best Fertilizer for Cucumbers? | Hunker. Hunker. https://www.hunker.com/13427375/what-is-the-best-fertil-izer-for-cucumbers

Bailey, V. (2018, December 15). What Not to Plant Near Cucumbers. Home Guides | SF Gate. https://homeguides.sfgate.com/not-plant-near-cucumbers-33318.html

Balogh, A. (n.d.). Garden Soil: How to Prepare Your Soil for a Garden - Garden Design. GardenDesign.com. Retrieved June 27, 2021, from https://www.gardendesign.com/soil/

Benefits of Community Growing. (n.d.). Www.edibleestates.co.uk. http://www.edibleestates.co.uk/benefits-of-community-growing/

Blando, M. (n.d.). How Much Sun Does a Cucumber Plant Need? Home-guides.sfgate.com. https://homeguides.sfgate.com/much-sun-cucumber-plant-need-52857.html

Boeckmann, C. (2021, March 25). Vegetable Gardening for Beginners. Old Farmer's Almanac. https://www.almanac.com/vegetable-gardening-for-beginners

Borge, A. (2014, April 24). The Financial Benefits of Starting a Vegetable Garden. DebtHelper.com. https://debthelper.com/blog/2014/04/fi-nancial-benefits-starting-vegetable-garden/

Campbell-Preston, C. (2016, September 12). Why Gardening is Great For Your Mental Health and Wellbeing | Capital Gardens. Capital Gardens. https://www.capitalgardens.co.uk/blog/gardening-great-mental-health-wellbeing/

Castillo, E. (2016, May 7). How much salad should you be eating each day? PCOSbites. https://pcosbites.com/2016/05/07/how-much-salad-should-you-be-eating-each-day/

Domoney, D. (2019a, March 8). Expert guide to soil. David Domoney. https://www.daviddomoney.com/expert-guide-to-soil/

Domoney, D. (2019b, March 11). Beginner's Guide to Growing Fruit and Veg. David Domoney. https://www.daviddomoney.com/beginners-guide-to-growing-fruit-and-veg/

Domoney, D. (2019c, May 13). Benefits of Gardening for Mental Health. David Domoney. https://www.daviddomoney.com/benefits-gardening-mental-health/

Druff, K. V. (2021, February 28). 8 Amazing Social Benefits of Gardening. Bunny's Garden. https://www.bunnysgarden.com/social-benefits-of-gardening/

Ferrandino, F. (2014, April 25). How to Prune Tomatoes. FineGardening. https://www.finegardening.com/article/pruning-tomatoes

Gardening: Invest in guaranteed growth in your own backyard. (2009, April). Cappersfarmer.com. https://www.cappersfarmer.com/yard-and-garden/gardening-invest-in-guaranteed-growth-in-your-own-backyard/

George, H. (2020, August 29). Identify, Prevent, and Treat Common Cabbage Diseases | Gardener's Path. Gardener's Path. https://gardenerspath.com/how-to/disease-and-pests/common-cabbage-diseases/

Gibson, A. (2012, November 27). Guide to Growing Spring Onions: Everything you need to know! The Micro Gardener. https://themicrogardener.com/guide-to-growing-spring-onions/

Gillihan, S. J. (2019, June 19). 10 Mental Health Benefits of Gardening | Psychology Today United Kingdom. Www.psychologytoday.com. https://www.psychologytoday.com/gb/blog/think-act-be/201906/10-mental-health-benefits-gardening

Go, G. (2014). 7 Surprising Financial Benefits of Gardening. US News & World Report; U.S. News & World Report. https://money.usnews.com/money/blogs/my-money/2014/05/07/7-surprising-financial-benefits-of-gardening

Growing Cabbages & General Cabbage Planting Tips. (n.d.). Bonnie Plants. https://bonnieplants.com/how-to-grow/growing-cabbage/#:~:text=Like%20most%20vegetables%2C%20cabbage%20needs

Hagen, L. (2019). 12 Gardening Tools to Buy - Essentials for Beginners - Garden Design. GardenDesign.com. https://www.gardendesign.com/how-to/tools.html

Haifa Group. (2018, March 11). Crop Guide: Tomato. Haifa Group. https://www.haifa-group.com/tomato-fertilizer/crop-guide-tomato

Hansen, J. (n.d.). The Easiest Fruits and Vegetables to Grow for Beginners. GardenTech.com. Retrieved July 11, 2021, from https://www.gardentech.com/blog/gardening-and-healthy-living/8-easy-to-grow-fruits-and-veggies

Harvard Health Publishing. (2018, August 13). Calories burned in 30 minutes for people of three different weights - Harvard Health. Harvard Health; Harvard Health. https://www.health.harvard.edu/diet-and-weight-loss/calories-burned-in-30-minutes-of-leisure-and-routine-activities

Hayes, K. (2017, June 14). 5 Health Benefits of Gardening and Planting. AARP. https://www.aarp.org/health/healthy-living/info-2017/health-benefits-of-gardening-fd.html

Heirloom Organics. (n.d.-a). How to Grow Cucumbers | Guide to Growing Cucumbers. Www.heirloom-Organics.com. Retrieved July 18, 2021, from http://www.heirloom-organics.com/guide/va/guidetogrowingcucumbers.html

Heirloom Organics. (n.d.-b). How to Grow Tomato | Guide to Growing Tomatoes. Www.heirloom-Organics.com. Retrieved July 17, 2021, from http://www.heirloom-organics.com/guide/va/guidetogrowingtomato.html

How to Grow Cabbage| Guide to Growing Cabbage. (n.d.). Www.heirloom-Organics.com. Retrieved August 2, 2021, from http://www.heirloom-organics.com/guide/va/guidetogrowingcabbage.html

How to Grow Carrots | Guide to Growing Carrots. (n.d.). Www.heirloom-Organics.com. Retrieved August 5, 2021, from http://www.heirloom-organics.com/guide/va/guidetogrowingcarrots.html

How to Grow Pepper | Guide to Growing Peppers. (n.d.). Www.heirloom-Organics.com. Retrieved August 5, 2021, from http://www.heirloom-organics.com/guide/va/guidetogrowingpeppers.html

How to Grow Radishes - Gardening Tips and Advice, Vegetable Seeds and Plants at Burpee.com. (2019). Burpee.com. https://www.burpee.com/gardenadvicecenter/vegetables/radishes/all-about-radishes/article10099.html

How to Grow Radishes | Guide to Growing Radishes. (n.d.). Www.heirloom-Organics.com. Retrieved August 5, 2021, from http://www.heirloom-organics.com/guide/va/guidetogrowingradish.html

Hutchins, R. (2017, October 31). 8 Surprising Health Benefits of Gardening | UNC Health Talk. UNC Health Talk. https://healthtalk.unchealthcare.org/health-benefits-of-gardening/

KJ Staff. (2020, November 25). What are the Different Methods of Sowing Seeds? Krishijagran.com. https://krishijagran.com/agripedia/what-are-the-different-methods-of-sowing-seeds/

Knerl, L. (2021, July 24). The True Cost Of Growing A Garden. Investopedia. https://www.investopedia.com/financial-edge/0312/the-true-cost-of-growing-a-garden.aspx

Larum, D. (2021, January 13). StackPath. Www.gardeningknowhow.com. https://www.gardeningknowhow.com/edible/vegetables/tomato/protecting-tomatoes-from-animals.htm

Leichty, C. (n.d.). Are Raised Garden Beds Better than In-Ground Garden Beds? Do Not Disturb Gardening. Retrieved June 26, 2021, from https://donotdisturbgardening.com/are-raised-garden-beds-better-than-in-ground-garden-beds/

Lobo, B. (2021, March 28). Growing Tomatoes From Seed: How, When and Ideal Temperatures. Dengarden - Home and Garden. https://dengarden.com/gardening/planting-tomato-seeds

Look, Z. (2020, January 31). Every Gardener Needs A Good Rake And Hoe. Hobby Farms. https://www.hobbyfarms.com/every-gardener-needs-a-good-rake-and-hoe/

Lussier, M. (2018, May 30). 5 Reasons To Grow Your Own Food. Healthy UNH. https://www.unh.edu/healthyunh/blog/nutrition/2018/05/5-reasons-grow-your-own-food

Maggie's Farm. (2020, May 20). Common Tomato Insects and How to Protect Your Plants. Maggie's Farm. https://maggiesfarmproducts.com/blogs/bug-help/tomato-pests

Mantel, S. (2019). Why are soils important? | ISRIC. Isric.org. https://www.isric.org/discover/about_soils/why-are-soils-important

Masley, S. (2019, October 4). How to Prepare the Soil for a Vegetable Garden. WikiHow. https://www.wikihow.com/Prepare-the-Soil-for-a-Vegetable-Garden

Max. (2020, July 5). 15 Different Types of Cucumbers That You Can Grow. Trees.com. https://www.trees.com/edible/cucumbers

Newcomb, L. (n.d.). Remedy for Nitrogen Overdose on Tomato Plants. Home Guides | SF Gate. https://homeguides.sfgate.com/remedy-nitrogen-overdose-tomato-plants-29733.html

Old Farmer's Almanac. (2017, August 12). Soil pH Levels for Plants. Old Farmer's Almanac. https://www.almanac.com/plant-ph

Old Farmer's Almanac. (2019, July 4). Radishes. Old Farmer's Almanac. https://www.almanac.com/plant/radishes

Palomo, E. (n.d.). Do Cucumbers Have Shallow Roots? Home Guides |

SF Gate. Retrieved July 18, 2021, from https://homeguides.sfgate.-com/cucumbers-shallow-roots-85473.html

Paul. (n.d.). Different types of gardens. Www.clausehomegarden.com. Retrieved June 26, 2021, from https://www.clausehomegarden.-com/rubrique-concept/resistances-aux-maladies/different-types-gardens

Pleasant, B. (2019, March 14). 8 Tips for Growing Tomatoes from Seed. GrowVeg. https://www.growveg.co.uk/guides/8-tips-for-growing-tomatoes-from-seed/

Quinn, L. (2016, April 26). The Benefits of Growing a Vegetable Garden. Burke Rehabilitation Hospital. https://www.burke.org/blog/2016/4/the-benefits-of-growing-a-vegetable-garden/83

Reilly, K. (2020, April 15). The Only Tools You Need to Start a Garden. EatingWell. https://www.eatingwell.com/article/17068/the-only-tools-you-need-to-start-a-garden/

Rhoades, H. (2021a, June 4). StackPath. Www.gardeningknowhow.com. https://www.gardeningknowhow.com/edible/vegetables/toma-to/watering-tomato-plants.htm

Rhoades, H. (2021b, June 29). StackPath. Www.gardeningknowhow.com. https://www.gardeningknowhow.com/edible/vegetables/toma-to/tomato-fertilizer.htm

Sanderson, S. (n.d.). How To Grow Tomatoes | Thompson & Morgan. Www.thompson-Morgan.com. Retrieved July 17, 2021, from https://www.thompson-morgan.com/how-to-grow-tomatoes

SCOTT, T. L., MASSER, B. M., & PACHANA, N. A. (2014). Exploring the health and well-being benefits of gardening for older adults. Ageing and Society, 35(10), 2176–2200. https://doi.org/10.1017/s0144686x14000865

Search | Garden Organic. (2016, February 9). Www.gardenorgan-ic.org.uk. http://www.gardenorganic.org.uk/sites/www.gardenor-ganic.org.uk/files/MIND

Sedghi, S. (2019, May 16). 10 Common Types of Tomatoes—and What to Do With Them. MyRecipes. https://www.myrecipes.com/ingredi-ents/types-of-tomatoes

Sherry, D. (2014, April 25). How to Harvest Tomatoes. FineGardening. https://www.finegardening.com/article/how-to-harvest-tomatoes

Sigler, J. (2009a, March 24). A Beginner's Guide to Fruit and Vegetable Gardening. SparkPeople. https://www.sparkpeople.com/re-source/nutrition_articles.asp?id=1292

Sigler, J. (2009b, March 24). A Beginner's Guide to Fruit and Vegetable

Gardening.   SparkPeople.   https://www.sparkpeople.com/re-source/nutrition_articles.asp?id=1292

Simons, L. A., Simons, J., McCallum, J., & Friedlander, Y. (2006). Lifestyle factors and risk of dementia: Dubbo Study of the elderly. Medical Journal of Australia, 184(2), 68–70. https://doi.org/10.5694/j.1326-5377.2006.tb00120.x

Singh, B. (2021, March 23). Sowing - An Overview and Different Methods of Sowing Seeds. BYJUS. https://byjus.com/biology/sowing/

Smith, C. (n.d.). Tomato Root Rot Due to Rain. Home Guides | SF Gate. Retrieved July 18, 2021, from https://homeguides.sfgate.-com/tomato-root-rot-due-rain-27887.html

Sowing, different types of sowing. (2017, July 28). Nature and Garden. https://www.nature-and-garden.com/gardening/sowing.html#

Stanborough, R. (2020, June 17). 10 Benefits of Gardening, Plus Helpful Tips & Recommendations. Healthline. https://www.healthline.-com/health/healthful-benefits-of-gardening#takeaway

Stross, A. (2016, January 28). How to Start a Garden on a Budget. Tenth Acre Farm. https://www.tenthacrefarm.com/how-to-start-a-garden-on-a-budget/

The benefits of gardening and food growing for health and well-being | Sustain. (2014, April 1). Www.sustainweb.org. https://www.sustain-web.org/publications/the_benefits_of_gardening_and_food_growing/

The Royal Horticultural Society. (2020). How to grow tomatoes / RHS Gardening.   Rhs.org.uk;   Royal   Horticultural   Society. https://www.rhs.org.uk/advice/grow-your-own/vegetables/tomatoes

The therapeutic properties of growing and gardening | Garden Organic. (n.d.). Www.gardenorganic.org.uk. Retrieved August 5, 2021, from https://www.gardenorganic.org.uk/therapeutic-properties-growing-and-gardening#:~:text=Mental%20health%20and%20well%2Dbeing

Thomas, C. (2021, June 29). Save Money By Growing Your Own Veg. Which?   https://www.which.co.uk/reviews/grow-your-own/arti-cle/growing-vegetables/save-money-by-growing-your-own-veg-a8zgZ4G3O3AC

Tilley, N. (2021, July 27). StackPath. Www.gardeningknowhow.com. https://www.gardeningknowhow.com/edible/vegetables/cucum-ber/when-to-pick-a-cucumber-how-to-prevent-yellow-cucum-bers.htm

Unusual Urban Planting: 5 Different Types of Gardening. (2008, July 9). WebUrbanist.   https://weburbanist.com/2008/07/09/5-different-types-of-gardening-unconventional-and-conventional-urban-planting/

Vinje, E. (2012, December 8). Beginner Tomato Gardening Guide. Planet Natural. https://www.planetnatural.com/tomato-gardening/

Boucher, E. (2022, October 9). Raised Vegetable Garden Bed Prevent Dogs. Vegetable Gardening News. https://www.vegetablegardeningnews.com/raised-vegetable-garden-bed-prevent-dogs/

Fruit and Veg. (n.d.). Scalpwood. Retrieved 3 November 2022, from https://scalpwood.com/fruit-and-veg.html

Garden Mantis. (2022, June 6). Gardening Tools List. https://gardenmantis.com/gardening-tools/

Gardening, I. (2022, October 8). How to Choose the Best Indoor Garden Kit. Indoor Gardening. https://indoorgardening.com/how-to-choose-the-best-indoor-garden-kit/

Gardening Tools Names: 35+ Essential Gardening Equipment with Pictures. (2022, May 2). Occupation Tools. https://occupationtools.com/gardening-tools-names/

Garlic Plant Temperature Tolerance: Ideal Temperature+Extreme. (2022, August 16). Nurserylady.com. https://nurserylady.com/garlic-plant-temperature-tolerance/

Growing Brussels Sprouts. (2020, May 29). Gardening Channel. https://www.gardeningchannel.com/growing-brussels-sprouts/

How to Grow Brussels Sprouts | Guide to Growing Brussels Sprouts. (n.d.). Retrieved 3 November 2022, from http://www.heirloom-organics.com/guide/va/guidetogrowingbrusselssprouts.html

Johnston, C. (2022, March 7). Best (and Worst) Onion Companion Plants. Growly. https://growfully.com/onion-companion-plants/

Max, C. (2022, August 19). Who has the best lawn care service - LAWNNNN [2022]. LAWNNNN. https://lawnnnn.com/who-has-the-best-lawn-care-service/

Sigler, J. S. C. (2009, March 24). A Beginner's Guide to Fruit and Vegetable Gardening. SparkPeople. https://www.sparkpeople.com/resource/nutrition_articles.asp?id=1292

What Tools Do I Need To Start a Vegetable Garden? (n.d.). Quickcrop UK. Retrieved 3 November 2022, from https://www.quickcrop.co.uk/blog/what-tools-do-i-need-to-start-a-vegetable-garden

Boucher, E. (2022, October 9). Raised Vegetable Garden Bed Prevent Dogs. Vegetable Gardening News. https://www.vegetablegardeningnews.com/raised-vegetable-garden-bed-prevent-dogs/

Fruit and Veg. (n.d.). Scalpwood. Retrieved 3 November 2022, from https://scalpwood.com/fruit-and-veg.html

Garden Mantis. (2022, June 6). Gardening Tools List. https://gardenman

tis.com/gardening-tools/

Gardening, I. (2022, October 8). How to Choose the Best Indoor Garden Kit. Indoor Gardening. https://indoorgardening.com/how-to-choose-the-best-indoor-garden-kit/

Gardening Tools Names: 35+ Essential Gardening Equipment with Pictures. (2022, May 2). Occupation Tools. https://occupationtools.com/gardening-tools-names/

Garlic Plant Temperature Tolerance: Ideal Temperature+Extreme. (2022, August 16). Nurserylady.com. https://nurserylady.com/garlic-plant-temperature-tolerance/

Johnston, C. (2022, March 7). Best (and Worst) Onion Companion Plants. Growfully. https://growfully.com/onion-companion-plants/

Max, C. (2022, August 19). Who has the best lawn care service - LAWNNNN [2022]. LAWNNNN. https://lawnnnn.com/who-has-the-best-lawn-care-service/

Peas: How to Grow It. (n.d.). SDSU Extension. Retrieved 3 November 2022, from https://extension.sdstate.edu/peas-how-grow-it

Sigler, J. S. C. (2009, March 24). A Beginner's Guide to Fruit and Vegetable Gardening. SparkPeople. https://www.sparkpeople.com/resource/nutrition_articles.asp?id=1292

What Tools Do I Need To Start a Vegetable Garden? (n.d.). Quickcrop UK. Retrieved 3 November 2022, from https://www.quickcrop.co.uk/blog/what-tools-do-i-need-to-start-a-vegetable-garden

10 Steps to Successfully Grow Your Own Kiwi Plant: A Personal Story and Expert Tips [Beginner-Friendly Guide]. (2023, April 25). Evilonions.com - Grow Plants. https://evilonions.com/10-steps-to-successfully-grow-your-own-kiwi-plant-a-personal-story-and-expert-tips-beginner-friendly-guide/

A Beginner's Guide to Fruit and Vegetable Gardening. (n.d.). SparkPeople. https://www.sparkpeople.com/resource/nutrition_articles.asp?id=1292

Admin. (2022a, June 3). How To Control Aphids On Strawberry Plants - Justagric. Justagric. https://justagric.com/how-to-control-aphids-on-strawberry-plants/

Admin. (2022b). How to Grow Pear Trees in 10 Simple Steps. The Gardening Dad. https://thegardeningdad.com/how-to-grow-pear-trees/

Admin. (2023, March 23). Growing Clematis Indoors In Pots: 11 Easy Growth Tips. INDOOR VEGETABLE GROWER. https://www.indoorvegetablegrower.com/growing-clematis-indoors-in-pots/

Amanda. (2023, May 1). PRUNING- A Vital Part of Plant Care - NSW

Northern Rivers News, Entertainment, Sports and Weather. NSW Northern Rivers News, Entertainment, Sports and Weather. https://thenorthernriverstimes.com.au/local-news/gardening/pruning-a-vital-part-of-plant-care/

Devenbwm, & Devenbwm. (2022). Choosing the Best Type of Soil for Your Backyard Garden | Berardi Irrigation. Berardi Irrigation | Small and Large Irrigation Systems. https://www.berardiirrigation.com/choosing-the-best-type-of-soil-for-your-backyard-garden/

Dickson, C. (2022). How to get rid of powdery mildew – for a healthier garden. homesandgardens.com. https://www.homesandgardens.com/gardens/how-to-get-rid-of-powdery-mildew

Disease-Resistant Apple Cultivars. (n.d.). MU Extension. https://extension.missouri.edu/publications/g6026

Duford, M. J. (2023, January 27). When to prune apple trees | Home for the Harvest. Home for the Harvest. https://www.homefortheharvest.com/when-to-prune-apple-trees/

Elrod, D. (2023, May 2). What Does Root Rot Look Like Pothos: A Quick Identification Guide - Foliage Friend - Learn About Different. Foliage Friend - Learn About Different Types of Plants. https://foliagefriend.com/what-does-root-rot-look-like-pothos/

FruitGuys. (2020). Fresh Fruit Storage and Ripening Tips. The FruitGuys. https://fruitguys.com/2012/07/fresh-fruit-storage-and-ripening-tips/

Gray mold in the flower garden. (n.d.). UMN Extension. https://extension.umn.edu/plant-diseases/gray-mold-flower-garden

Growing a Gourmet Garden. (n.d.). Portugal Farm Experience. https://www.portugalfarmexperience.com/blog/growing-a-gourmet-garden/

Insectek. (2023). 11 Common Pests and Bugs to look out for in Arizona. Insectek Pest Solutions. https://www.insectekpest.com/blog/common-pests-to-watch-for-in-arizona/

Johnston, A. (2023). The Essential Guide to Saving Strawberry Seeds for Planting. ShunCy. https://shuncy.com/article/how-to-save-strawberry-seeds

Kimberly. (2023). Companion Planting: A Guide To Successful Plant Pairings. Backyard Homestead HQ. https://backyardhomesteadhq.com/companion-planting-a-guide-to-successful-plant-pairings/

Managing Spider Mites on Houseplants. (n.d.). UMN Extension. https://extension.umn.edu/news/managing-spider-mites-houseplants

Move, O. W. O. (2023, January 25). Do all Ficus trees have invasive roots?

Remodel Or Move. https://www.remodelormove.com/do-all-ficus-trees-have-invasive-roots/

Nelson, T. (2023, April 27). 13 Fruit Trees That Grow In Zone 8 - The Garden Magazine. The Garden Magazine. https://thegarden magazine.com/13-fruit-trees-that-grow-in-zone-8/

Organic Growers School. (2018, October 19). Watering Your Garden | Organic Growers School. https://organicgrowersschool.org/garden ers/library/watering-your-garden/

Pruning Deciduous Fruit Trees - Gardening Solutions - University of Flor-ida, Institute of Food and Agricultural Sciences. (n.d.). https://gar-deningsolutions.ifas.ufl.edu/care/pruning/pruning-deciduous-fruit-trees.html

Raspberries: Leaves have a white powder on them | Berry Diagnostic Tool. (n.d.). https://blogs.cornell.edu/berrytool/raspberries/raspber ries-leaves-have-a-white-powder-on-them/

Reinhardt, A. (n.d.). Choosing a Nursery (Tips.Net). Sharon Parq Associates, Inc. https://gardening.tips.net/ T005083_Choosing_a_Nursery.html

Saleem, I. (2023, February 28). **How To Grow Fruit Trees From Seeds?** . Slick Garden. https://slickgarden.com/how-to-grow-fruit-trees-from-seeds/

Soil - Fixing Food. (2023, April 28). Fixing Food. https://fixingfood. humanitarianchangemakers.net/directory/soil/

Strawberry. (2022). Strawberry Plant: The Complete Guide. Strawberry Plants. https://strawberryplants.org/strawberry-plant/

Suits, P., & Suits, P. (2023). The Benefits of Using Companion Planting in Your Garden. Pea Suits. https://peasuits.com/the-benefits-of-using-companion-planting-in-your-garden.html

Taylor, G., & Taylor, G. (2022a). The Dos and Don'ts of Watering Plants. Bob Vila. https://www.bobvila.com/articles/watering-plants/

Taylor, G., & Taylor, G. (2022b). The Dos and Don'ts of Watering Plants. Bob Vila. https://www.bobvila.com/articles/watering-plants/

The Free Range Life. (2022). 8 Simple Ways to Improve Your Garden Soil for Free Story. The Free Range Life®. https://thefreerangelife.com/ web-stories/8-simple-ways-to-improve-your-garden-soil-for-free-story/

Turner, B. (2019). Can You Answer These Agriculture Questions a Farmer Should Know? HowStuffWorks. https://play.howstuffworks.com/ quiz/can-you-answer-these-agriculture-questions-a-farmer-should-know

Velez, B. (2023a). Propagating Persimmons: A Step-by-Step Guide. ShunCy. https://shuncy.com/article/how-to-propagate-persimmon

Velez, B. (2023b). Timing is Key: Pruning Your Apricot Tree for Optimal Growth. ShunCy. https://shuncy.com/article/when-is-the-best-time-to-prune-an-apricot-tree

VNC Web Services, https://www.virtualnightclub.net/. (n.d.). Growing Vegetables All Year Round in a Walipini - Article - A Gardeners Forum. A Gardeners Forum. https://www.agardenersforum.com/article/view/6/growing-vegetables-all-year-round-in-a-walipini.html

W, E. (2023a). 10 Delicious Ways to Make the Best Strawberry Cake Ever - cookindocs.com. cookindocs.com. https://cookindocs.com/best-cake-for-strawberries/

W, E. (2023b). 7 Surprising Benefits of Eating Grapes at the Right Time - cookindocs.com. cookindocs.com. https://cookindocs.com/best-time-to-eat-grape/

WebMD Editorial Contributors. (2020, September 14). Health Benefits of Green Apples. WebMD. https://www.webmd.com/diet/health-benefits-green-apples

Zahariadis, J. (2023, February 25). How to Grow Cilantro - Garden for Beginners. Garden for Beginners. https://gardenforbeginners.com/how-to-grow-cilantro/

www.ingramcontent.com/pod-product-compliance
Lightning Source LLC
Chambersburg PA
CBHW031954040426
42448CB00006B/355